Death in a Hansom Cab; the 1904 Persecution of Nan Patterson.

by
Kerry Segrave

CONTENTS.

INTRODUCTION.

The subject of this book is the mysterious death of a bookmaker and somewhat prominent figure in horse racing circles by the name of Frank Thomas (Caesar) Young. On Saturday morning June 4, 1904 Young was a passenger in a hansom cab that was being driven along Broadway Avenue in New York City. Close to 9:00 AM a shot rang out and Young was dead within minutes. There was only one other person riding with Young in that horse-drawn taxi that morning, and that was Ann Elizabeth Patterson, better known as Nan Patterson. Initially the belief was that Young had died as a result of suicide. However quickly suspicion turned to the only other person in the vehicle. Soon Nan Patterson found herself charged with murder in the first degree. She was taken into custody that day and would not taste freedom again for over 11 months. After three trials on first degree murder charges no conviction was registered against the woman.

What happened in those trials, and in the trial by media that Nan endured over all that time, was less concerned with looking at the "facts" upon which to convict or not convict Patterson, and much more concerned with other items. Nan had been an actor on stage for about two years or a little less and had attained no great notice or public attention from her appearances. However, public sentiment was snobbish toward the acting profession and looked upon the females within the field as "loose" and generally immoral. Nan was on trial for that. She was the lover of Thomas, a married man, and she was on trial for that, the concept of home wrecker being in play. As an actor she lived an unconventional life by the rigid and puritanical standards of the day, and she was tried for that. More that a few editorials came out to say in no uncertain terms that Nan deserved punishment for reasons of lifestyle as much as for anything. The state's case was based on no evidence at all, merely lies, allegations and fanciful and bizarre theories. There should have been a fast and easy acquittal, most observers felt that would be the outcome, before the event. However, it was a draw, twice (the first mistrial was due to a juror going down with illness to the point that he could not continue). Apparently, many in the juries also subscribed to the idea that Patterson needed to be punished for lifestyle.

Media coverage was often appallingly bad with smear after smear appearing in print against the woman. Interviews with Nan that never took place and quotations from Nan appeared in print, ascribed to those interviews that never took place. This book is about the persecution of a young woman by a patriarchal system wherein the full and brutal misogyny of that system was on display. Nan was not officially punished as a direct result of her trials but she was punished in other ways and her life disintegrated following her release, as the morally upright and uptight looked on with glee.

Research for this book was done using online databases with the Library of Congress' "Chronicling America" being the most useful, Also used were newspaperarchive.com and various other online newspaper databases.

Chapter one looks at the backgrounds of both Charles Thomas (Caesar) Randolph and Ann Elizabeth Patterson, known as Nan Patterson. As well it traces their relationship from their first meeting in July 1902, perhaps a bit later that year, up to and including that fateful June 4 1904 day when the tragic shooting occurred. By the end of that day and by the end of that chapter Nan was incarcerated and would not see the outside world for almost a year. Initially she was held as a witness and a bail amount was given. However, as the course of the investigation would show, the state had no intention of ever allowing Patterson out on bail, and it never did.

In chapter two the investigation is outlined, an investigation that led to Nan being indicted for murder. It was a weak and very biased investigation. The state fairly quickly decided Nan was guilty of murder and set about to find the "facts" to prove that contention. Since no such facts existed the state was reduced to having people, all biased against Nan, step forward to make outrageous claims and exaggerations, all lies. It was at this time that the first of the "eye-witnesses" came forward to swear they had seen it all. For the better part of a year they came out of the woodwork, one after another, all spouting nonsense. No one had seen the shooting. The closest person was the cab driver. And, like all such drivers, he sat at the back, outside the passenger compartment, the roof of which prevented him from seeing into that compartment. The "trap" which allowed money and verbal instructions to go back and forth between driver and passengers was closed as it usually was. The driver had not seen the shooting but he had seen that there was no one on the street close enough to see anything. Nevertheless the media played up such nonsense, alternating those account with smear stories about Nan. Such a vamp was the woman, if the nonsense was to be believed, that, over just a few short years, three or was it four men committed suicide because they were in great despair when Nan rejected them as suitors. But it was all nonsense.

Efforts at bail intensified, as outlined in chapter three, as the case moved from a murder indictment to the eve of the first trial. The following two chapters look at trial number one and trial number two, with very little time between the two events. Both were mistrials with trial number one ending when a juror's sudden illness prevented him from continuing. There was no alternate juror system in place at the time and for a verdict to be registered and have the force of law it needed a 12 to zero vote. Trial number two ended with six in favor of conviction and six in favor of acquittal.

Chapter six investigates the time after trial number two. So much foot dragging was displayed by the state in refusing to set a date for the next trial that a sitting judge in another court was appealed to and that judge ordered the state to set a trial date, or release the defendant on bail. It was during this time that more and more time and attention was devoted to Nan's sister Julia Morgan and her husband J. Morgan Smith. It was here that the state hatched a theory that became more and more bizarre in which the Smiths had conspired with Nan to extort money from Caesar Young, as the state prosecutors more and more entered the fantasy land inhabited by seemingly endless "eye-witnesses," who never stopped coming.

The final trial, number three, also ended in a hung jury, with the official last ballot count never released. The other fantasy that the state more and more came to rely on also failed completely in this trial. That was the idea that Morgan Smith bought the weapon used in the shooting, on Friday June 3, the day before the tragedy. The pawnbroker who claimed he sold the weapon made about ten attempts to identify one or another of the Smiths, Nan herself, and Caesar Young. Some of those attempts were made in open court, some behind the scenes in jails, and some from photographs. Never could he identify anybody.

Even after the third mistrial the state was reluctant to release Nan. It was obvious that a fourth trial would not take place but the prosecutor was slow to release her, as detailed in chapter 8.

Chapter nine follows the rest of Nan Patterson's story, at least as far as it was ever publicly reported, and that was into the early 1920s. She continued to be hounded and smeared by the press. An attempt to return to the stage was a quick and brutal failure, and her personal life also unraveled. The story of Nan Patterson is the story of a brutal, misogynistic persecution of a young woman by an infuriated patriarchy, under the guise of prosecution.

An apparent publicity shot of the Floradora sextet in one of the road company troupes of that production. Nan Patterson (then known as Nan Randolph) is second from the right. The year would have been 1901-1902.

CHAPTER 1. THE DEATH AND THE INCARCERATION.

On Saturday morning June 10, 1904, at some time between 8:00 AM and 9:00 AM a hansom cab was traveling along West Broadway in New York City. Motorized taxis were just beginning to make their appearance in various parts of the world but this one, as the vast majority were, was horse-drawn by a single animal. The driver was located outside of the cab itself, on a raised seat behind the cab. The roof of the cab provided some shelter for the passengers from the elements and that meant that the driver could not see what was going on in the cab. Three passengers could sometimes be squeezed into the cab but it usually carried just one or two. The roof contained a small trap door opening (just called a "trap,") which could be opened by either the passenger or the driver. The trap was used to easily allow money to pass back and forth and for the flow of verbal instructions, which otherwise might be muffled or unheard if the trap was closed. In this particular hansom on this particular morning the vehicle carried two passengers. One of them was Frank Thomas Young a bookmaker who was about 40 years old, and married. The other was Ann Elizabeth Patterson who was also married, but separated. She went by the name of Nan Patterson, was 21 years old, and had enjoyed a brief theatrical career although without gaining much notice or attention. During her brief time on the stage she used the name of Nan Randolph. The couple were lovers and had been so, off and on, over the previous couple of years. The hansom cab was heading toward the New York pier where Young (known by the nickname "Caesar") was scheduled to meet his wife and from where the pair were slated to catch an ocean liner for a trip to Europe that would keep the couple out of America for at least a few months. Young's family, not just his wife but also his siblings and in-laws had all worked on Caesar to badger and cajole him to take the trip abroad and hopefully, at least from their point of view, put an end to the relationship. Thus, during that cab ride the couple must have been conflicted. At about the point where the cab met the cross street of Franklin Avenue, a shot rang out. The driver saw nothing, unsurprisingly. There were no witnesses to the event – excluding the various liars who would pop up over the following weeks and months and swear they had seen the whole thing. Unfortunately, the media often treated such people as serious witnesses. It should have been a straightforward case for the police; two people in a space unpopulated by others, one gun, one shot fired. How many situations were possible? But it was not a simple matter for the police. What followed was a poor investigation, a poor prosecution, multiple trials conducted in the media and by the media, with the explicit and/or implicit help of the authorities. It was also a sexist investigation and a prosecution operated by the patriarchy with its gloves off. The result was the arrest, indictment and trial of Patterson on a murder charge, despite the fact there was no evidence whatsoever; there was nothing but a sexist desperation on the part of an incompetent and vindictive district attorney's office. Nan was tried three times and three times there was a mistrial.

Caesar Young was mentioned in brief items in the newspapers as early as 1897. At the start of that year a brief article appeared showing how the horsemen at New Orleans were faring financially. Eleven stables were listed, being those stables whose horses had won no less than $1,000 during the previous week. Top grosser was Avondale stable at $3,693 while Caesar Young was listed at number 10 out of the 11, with a gross of $1,397.

Later in that year it was reported that racing men were beginning to arrive in San Francisco for the winter season at the Ingleside track. One of those who had just arrived was Caesar Young, bringing with him about 12 horses.

From then on Young appeared to spend most, if not all, of his professional life as a horseman in California, centered on Oakland. In May 1901 a scandal was reported to be brewing in the Butchers' Board of Trade over the action of the committee in charge of the racing in Oakland on butchers' day in allotting the betting privilege to bookmaker Caesar Young for a sum that was just one-half of that offered separately by both Harry Corbett and George Rose. Apparently the practice of formal bids for the betting concession was dropped and the concession awarded directly to Young by the chair of that committee, one John H. McMenomy.

A full page of noted gambling figures in the San Francisco area appeared in a San Francisco newspaper. That page featured caricature drawings of 13 of those men. Caesar Young was then well known enough in San Francisco racing circles that he was one of the men who who was deemed worthy of meriting a caricature likeness.

At the very end of 1903 another racing scandal was said to have been in the air in the San Francisco area horse racing circles. This time the board of racing stewards was reportedly investigating a complaint laid by a former jockey and then seconded by a valet for another jockey. The charge laid in those complaints was that Young had instructed the second jockey to deliberately lose a race.

The only news item linking Young and Patterson before that fateful June 4 1904 appeared in a San Francisco paper on March 2 1904. What was described as a "sensation" in racing circles the day before was the reported disappearance of Young, who had been missing from his usual spot at the track on the two previous days and, noted the reporter; "Coupled with his disappearance is a story of his infatuation for a pretty member of the original *Floradora* sextet, who seemed to have completely turned his head." Having missed being at the track on the Monday and Tuesday, he last sighting was on the Sunday when he was spotted in a restaurant with Randolph, but missing since then (the paper published its item on Wednesday). According to the article the Randolph woman "has been the central figure in several escapades," both in this city and Los Angeles."

The couple had gone to Los Angeles for a few days and the whole affair was brought to a head during that time with Mrs. Young suddenly turning up, accompanied by a few relatives. It was then that Mrs. Young began to lay out plans, aided by her relatives, to take Caesar out of America to Europe to try and end the affair. It was during that time the was groundwork was laid for the tragedy that would ensue on June 4. Even in that brief item the media was getting its "facts" about Nan wrong and beginning its program of character assassination. Nan was never a member of the original *Floradora* stage production, but a member of one of the traveling companies formed up to take advantage of the success that the original production enjoyed in New York City. Her "escapades" were greatly exaggerated by the press or, more often, simply invented.

Nan Patterson also received a few mentions in print prior to June 4 1904. A brief note that appeared on September 15 1901 listed the names of the principals engaged to present the play *Floradora* through the west; that is, one of the road companies was being formed at this time. Nine of the principals were listed as well as a list of the six names of the women who would sing the sextet, one of which was Nan Randolph (Patterson). The sextet in *Floradora* was a sort of glorified chorus, with more work to do in the production.

Another mention of Nan came in March 1903 when she was staying in a San Francisco hotel. According to the article she put too much trust in a hotel bellboy by the name of John Carrage. In the hotel she gave Carrage $200 to buy her a train ticket and while the bellboy left with her money he never returned to the hotel. Said a reporter; Nan Randolph "a young lady well known in Los Angeles" was a victim of "misplaced confidence in the honesty of a bellboy." Randolph had arrived in San Francisco a few days earlier on her way to New York City and was staying at the Victoria Hotel on Geary Street while she made arrangements for her trip. Two days after her arrival she gave Carrage $200 to get the ticket (with sleeper accommodation) and to also pay some small bills that she had incurred around town. He never came back. When she checked with the railroad she discovered that no ticket had been purchased in her name. Carrage had been employed at the hotel for just three days at the time he disappeared with Nan's money. Patterson purchased a ticket herself and left San Francisco a day later.

While her performances in *Floradora* do no seem to have garnered any critical reviews or notices she had enough fame that her divorce made the newspapers. Ann Elizabeth Martin (Nan's married name) was granted a divorce on April 30, 1903 in San Francisco by Judge Graham, from Leon Gaines Martin on the grounds of desertion and failure to provide. She had met Martin in 1898, when she was just 16 years old, in Baltimore and married him in that city. in November 1898. For some months, reportedly, they lived happily and then according to "Mrs. Martin's testimony" her husband started drinking and gambling. Them he grew neglectful, despite her protests and failed "to keep her supplied with means of support." It was then she determined to utilize her vocal powers and fine presence as a means of obtaining the sustenance her wealthy husband denied her." It would later be revealed that Caesar Young had urged her to get a divorce and that he paid the costs involved. In this account after her separation from Martin she secured a position as one of the members of the sextet in the *Floradora* company organized by Edna Wallace Hopper, that was in July 1901. Nan stayed with that company and toured in the west until that group disbanded, perhaps in 1902. She then came to San Francisco and took up residence with her sister Julia Patterson, with whom she had been living for the previous year, long enough to give the local divorce courts jurisdiction "over her matrimonial difficulties." That meant Nan took up residence in San Francisco no later than April 1902.

There were a number of mentions in various papers about a Floradora company that toured the west during the appropriate period and it was probably the company Patterson was affiliated with, although it was not certain, as no names were mentioned. The company played in Salt Lake City for three days in September 1901; it played in Paducah Kentucky on January 21 1902; and the play made its first appearance in Savannah Georgia in the middle of February 1902 and garnered good reviews at that city.

Nan's fame as an actor, albeit brief and lacking much public notice, arose from her part in *Floradora*, an Edwardian musical comedy. It opened in London England in 1899 and after a long and successful run there it debuted on Broadway in New York City in 1900, and enjoyed a long and successful run there. The book was written by Jimmy Davis (under the alias Owen Hall). It was so popular that Broadway revivals were held in 1902, 1905 and 1920. A good portion of its success was attributed to the Floradora Girls (the sextet), who were once described as a "sextette of tall, gorgeous damsels, clad in pink walking costumes, black picture hats and carrying frilly parasols." Fairly rigid physical standards were imposed and the chosen girls had to be 5' 4" tall and weigh 130 pounds. [A walking costume was simply what the average female of the time wore when she went walking to the store or out to visit friends. All people of the time wore hats and the first decade of the 1900s would become well known for the gigantic hats that females adopted, or had foisted upon them by fashion, and those hats became known as "picture" hats. The sextet were little more than chorus girls elevated slightly as they had more to do in the production; that is, songs]. Those girls were subject to much popular adoration and had many male admirers. The six original sextet members of the original Broadway production [not Nan's] were said to have all married well financially.

Several years later, in 1907, an article appeared that claimed a new type of show girl emerged because of *Floradora*. Prior to

Floradora the chorus girl wore the same kind of fleshings [flesh-colored tights] that had been in vogue since the days when *The Black Crook* first shocked the country. That later production debuted in 1866 in New York City and featured a chorus of 70 females attired in skimpy costumes and skin-colored tights. That introduced sex appeal into stage productions, through the chorus girl, and things changed little until *Floradora* arrived. According to the 1907 piece a metamorphosis took place; "The show girl was lifted to a pedestal such as she had never occupied before. Diamonds, automobiles flowers, Wall Street winnings and millionaire husbands were proffered to her." What Hall did was to declare that beauty unadorned was not necessarily beauty most adored so he began giving the chorus girl some clothes. In place of the traditional tights the chorus girls were given expensive gowns and hats. He also gave them a song and a huge fan base developed. That original New York City production spawned as many as half a dozen touring road companies [one of which contained Nan as a member].

Morally speaking, the chorus girls, and actresses in general, were held low esteem. Back in the time of *The Black Crook* females were infrequently seen at live productions, at least those meant for the masses. Audience members were mostly male and were raucous and rowdy, smoking and drinking in the seats and generally running riot. Females appeared on the stage, as main performers in acts, in secondary roles in acts and, always, as chorus girls. The few females in the audiences were mostly prostitutes, literally, who worked the male crowd for business. Females generally avoided being audience members in such uninviting surroundings. Over time the theatre owners improved the standards, physically cleaned up their venues, and so forth, mainly in order to attract that half of the population that hardly ever attended – women. Perhaps attracted by the low reputation of stage females a new character showed up – the theatre sexual harasser – or, as he was called in that era, the stage door Johnny. An article that appeared in 1895 noted that several theatre managers in New York City had decided to put a stop to the gathering of stage door Johnnies about their stage doors after performances and had engaged men to "attend to the matter. Men with clubs." These Johnnies hung around outside the stage doors after shows in order to harass emerging female players from the production to annoy them, to harass them, and to attempt to pick them up. One description of them was that; "they speak with no good motive. They are not gentlemen and they are cowards." After the Young death a friend of Nan's mentioned that Patterson often stayed extra late after a show finished specifically to avoid that unpleasant stage door crowd.

One of the best known Broadway impresarios in American history was Florenz Ziegfeld Jr. He published an article in 1921 declaring that the stage door Johnnies had disappeared from the scene. In writing about them he also remarked on the reputation of chorus girls saying people; "take it for granted that chorus girls are a fast set, never happy unless they are flying off on some giddy joy ride to a gay cafe where champagne is secretly uncorked and a general wild orgy ensues." Ziegfeld also noted that chorus girls of the time were mostly decoration and paid poorly. They tried to survive on little money and at the same time advance themselves professionally and thus, he thought, who could blame them for accepting meal offers from the Johnnies, and so forth. Around 1900 he said a typical chorus girl was paid about $22 a week and was compelled to purchase the shoes, stockings and tights used in the production. Then she had to clothe herself and pay room and board and all her other expenses out of a net pay of perhaps $17 to $18 a week. The impresario noted a belief that was held, in 1921 and earlier, about the chorus girl, namely; "A large class of people still cling to the belief that any girl – no matter how well behaved she may be or how sterling a character she may appear – must be shunned if she has been in a chorus."

An article that appeared in print in 1904 had the headline; "Can a moral, upright chorus girl succeed?" That article came about, it was said, as the result of a large number of letters received by a newspaper on the subject. And, concluded the piece, about those queried on the issue; "All were unanimous in saying that a young woman who tries to lead a moral upright life cannot succeed as a chorus girl." It was images such as the above that Nan carried with her, perhaps unbeknownst to her, as she tangled with America's so-called justice system and as she dealt with a rigid patriarchal order that came down with force on all women and with extra force on all women it defined as morally deficient. Thus Nan would be viewed and portrayed in the media as little more than a home-wrecking "loose" woman. When it came to women and the justice system the first order of business for the patriarchy was always, and remained, blame the woman herself.

And then it was June 4 1904, a little after 9:00 AM. Frank (Caesar) Young was dead; Nan Patterson was beside herself with grief; and Mrs. Young was standing on a pier in New York City beside an ocean liner waiting to board for the couple's trip to Europe, and wondering why Caesar had not arrived at the pier. Officials were on their way there to deliver the tragic news. The police were confused and would remain so for the duration. Forensics conducted an abysmal investigation which, of course, fed the police confusion, and an inept ,misogynistic district attorney stood by, waiting to add his bumbling to the growing pile.

Many reports of the death of Young appeared in the press on that June 4th day, with the earliest ones declaring the death to have been the result of suicide; that is, Caesar shot himself to death due to the coming breakup of his affair with Patterson, even if that separation only lasted the few months the Youngs planned to spend in Europe. Many of those early accounts were littered with errors. One newspaper from Salem Oregon declared that Frank Young, a "well-known bookman shot and killed himself in a cab this morning while proceeding up Broadway with Mrs. Nan Patterson. It was thought he was heavily hit financially in the book recently. The account declared that

Nan was a member of the original *Floradora* sextet and that she was being held by the police. According to this account Patterson "hysterically" told the authorities that Young had told her nothing of the trip abroad until that very morning and that just before he fired the shot he told her he would be gone several months and might never see her again.

Another account that rushed into print with the death as a suicide described Caesar as "the best known horseman and bookmaker who ever operated in California and for the last few summers he had had control of the betting at the race meetings in Oregon and Washington..." Young and his wife were said to have lived in a fine residence in Claremont, a suburb of Oakland. A few months earlier the racing people at Oakland were surprised one day at the sudden disappearance of Young. A few days later he was reported to be in Los Angeles and had gone from San Francisco with a "chorus girl." Calling a woman a "chorus girl" was a slur on her morals and it placed the recipient of such an insult at a level not much above that of prostitute. Herein "Mrs. Patterson" was also incorrectly described as a member of the original *Floradora* sextet, and that she was being held by the police. Many early accounts referred to Nan as "Mrs. Patterson, even though she had been divorced over a year before the death of Young. And, if her married name was to be used it should have been Mrs. Martin. The use of an erroneous married name to describe her likely was done by the press to reinforce the idea of adultery and the "improper" morality of the woman involved. Since she had reverted to her birth name after the divorce the appropriate address in the press would have been Miss Nan Patterson, but that way the immediate inference of adultery was not obvious. Men in San Francisco who knew Young refused to believe he killed himself on account of any loses at the races, stated a reporter; "They think heavy drinking and domestic troubles due to escapades with various women caused his suicide." This journalist went on to speculate that it was known that the woman he took with him to Los Angeles [March 1904] followed him to New York City [May 1904] "and word from the east some time ago says   that he was badly worried by her presence there. Another story is that he was madly in love with the woman and dreaded a separation."

When the case was reported in another newspaper as a suicide the journalist noted that; "the shrieks of a female occupant of the [hansom] rig aroused the police. Young died within minutes of being shot and the screams of the woman with him alerted the police. "Mrs." Patterson was described herein as a "former actress" and that she was being held by the police as a witness owing to the "conflicting evidence," on $5,000 bail.

When a paper from Topeka Kansas covered the event it also stated unequivocally that death was the result of a suicide. The first police office on the scene found Caesar bleeding from a wound in the chest. The man's head was in the woman's lap and she was screaming hysterically. Nan was said to have told the officer that Young had told her he was going to Europe and he might or might not see her in the future. Then, said Patterson, Young drew a revolver and shot himself. Patterson and the cab driver were then taken to the police station. Young was described herein as an Englishman by birth who was brought to the United States around 1890 by the old Manhattan Club, as a representative amateur athlete of England. Several years later Caesar moved on and began to buy race horses.

Later in the day, on June 4, accounts of the tragedy became more mixed as to the cause of Young's death. One account noted in its headline; "Horseman killed riding in a hack," while a subhead was more slanted, and proclaimed; "Death of Frank T. Young is charged to Miss Nan Patterson an actress." At least her name was published correctly.

A lengthy account in a Salt Lake City Utah newspaper called the event, in its headline; "A case of suicide or murder?" Caesar was called a bookmaker, horse owner and stockholder in Pacific Coast race tracks. He was shot and killed in a hansom cab on his way to the White Star Line pier to join his wife and sail to Europe. At first the death was reported as suicide but various circumstances caused the police to later change their views.

With Young in the cab was "Mrs." Nan Patterson "formerly an actress whose stage name was Nan Randolph and who was said to be a member of the original *Floradora* sextet." She told police Young shot himself after announcing to her he was going to Europe to be probably gone for several months. The police told the coroner, however, the revolver was in the man's pocket and that he did not believe Young could have put it there after shooting himself. Patterson was taken to a police station where she "collapsed." At the station Young's business partner, a man named John D. Millin stopped in. He stated that Young never carried a revolver and that he did not believe death was due to a self-inflicted wound. Millin said that Young, who came here from England 10 to 15 years ago, a poor man, was worth, at the time of his death, more than $500,000. When Millin and Patterson came in sight of each other in the station he tried to assault Nan, but was held back by police officers. When she was with the coroner, Patterson told him she was a niece of the cashier of a leading New York bank. She said she heard a muffled report right after Young told her he was going to leave her. She said she did not see any pistol and that she thought he shot himself with the pistol in his coat pocket. At least that was what the account stated that Nan told the coroner. Bail for Patterson was first fixed at $1,000 while she was being held as a witness. But then later on that same day, June 4, it was increased to $5,000, by the coroner at the request of the police officials.

The most comprehensive account of that first day came from a New York City publication. "Mrs. Nan Patterson" was described as a niece of Charles Patterson, cashier of the Fourth National Bank. At Hudson Street Hospital where Young was taken, although dead, letters were found, it was claimed, in his pocket, according to police, from Patterson "and written in a threatening manner." [There were no such letters]. According to this piece Nan was held without bail and sent to the Tombs municipal jail (formally known as the Manhattan Detention Complex). Young and Patterson had started that fateful cab ride at around 8:00 AM on the Saturday morning. The two engaged the hansom operated by Fred Michaels at Columbus Circle and told Michaels to drive them to the pier, where Young was slated to sail on the White Star liner Germanic. At the time Nan was living at the St. Paul Hotel, very near Columbus Circle. Michaels was said herein to have told the police that nothing of importance occurred on the way downtown until arriving at Franklin Street and West Broadway, where he was compelled to stop to let a string of teams pass. Allegedly he heard Young say to Patterson; "Well, Nan, I've got to go away for two or three months. I may not see you again. In fact, I don't think I will ever see you again. It's better that I should not." In the next instance the cabman said he heard a pistol shot and knew that either the man or the woman had been shot. A nearby policeman had his attention drawn to the commotion and discovered the man's body lying across the woman's lap and a revolver in the pocket of the man. The "conversation" between the two reported earlier in the paragraph never took place. It was completely false. Michaels, as he later testified heard nothing at all, except for a gunshot. When Young's body was searched it was reported that it contained $1,820 in cash and a considerable amount of diamond jewelry. His wife had the tickets to Europe with staterooms on the Germanic reserved in the name of Mr. and Mrs. Caesar Young. Waiting at the pier with Mrs. Young was John Millin and William Luce (a brother-in-law of Caesar). They were all on the White Star Line pier when news of the shooting was taken to them "by reporters." Mrs. Young returned to her hotel after hearing the news while Millin rushed to the police station and tried to attack Nan, charging her with killing Young.

In her statement to the coroner Patterson said that her sister Julia with whom she lived at the St. Paul Hotel (Julia was Mrs. J. Morgan Smith and Nan lived with Mr. and Mrs. J. Morgan Smith at that hotel) received a telephone message from Caesar at 7:30 AM that morning. Young told Julia to have Nan meet him at Columbus Circle at 8:00 AM. Nan got there at 8:05 to find Young waiting. During the cab ride heading to the pier the pair stopped once or twice to enter a bar for a drink. Young told Nan he was going to meet his wife at the pier and she was to get out of the cab a few blocks before the cab arrived there. During the ride he told her he was sorry but he did not think that after that day he would be able to ever see her again. As they were talking she heard a pistol shot that was muffled and as she turned Caesar fell over in her lap. Nan continued her statement by stated she first met Young three years earlier on her way to California. She had met him frequently since then and admitted she had been "intimate" with him. They came together on the train from California to New York City five weeks earlier as far as Chicago. Young then took one train to New York City while Patterson took another train to Washington D.C., to visit her family for a few days before continuing on to New York. Said Nan; "I loved him dearly and he told me he loved me. I believe he killed himself because he was made despondent through his love for me." She admitted taking the gun from his pocket and then putting it back. Millin, in his statement smeared Nan with more false facts. He said; "I knew this woman in California. She was in love with an actor in a *Ben Hur* company when she was with the *Floradora* company. He became insane over her and committed suicide in her presence. Another lover of hers on the coast killed himself. All of Young's friends had been trying to get him to give up this woman. He would go away and she would follow him. Young told me that she secured much money from him." Millin added that he was with Young until 1:00 AM on the morning of June 4. He was in good humor and said he was going to Europe to get away from Patterson and that his object in going to Europe was that he she could hardly follow him there. Everything Millin was credited with saying was false but all of such material likely helped to blacken Nan's reputation and standing in public and tilt the scales of "justice" against her. Later in the morning of June 4 Caesar Young awoke in the residence of Luce, where he and his wife had been staying since their arrival in New York City, a month or so earlier. He told his wife that he was going out to get shaved. She replied that she would meet him at the pier. Captain Langan of the New York Police Department declared he had been informed that some "valuable letters" had been found in the dead man's pockets that will "go far toward proving that he did not commit suicide." However, he admitted the police did not then "have custody of those letters." Perhaps, because those letters did not exist.

At that point the first day of the tragedy, June 4, came to any end. Nan Patterson was incarcerated in the Tombs and, unbeknownst to her, would not see freedom for almost a full year. In theory she could have been released by posting bail. However, the state had no intention of ever allowing bail. Reports about the case on the second day, June 5, were similar to that of the first day. Some of those reports actually were datelined the 4th. There was more false and/or exaggerated news and there was more smearing of Nan Patterson. It was trial by the press as a case that had initially been viewed as suicide was rapidly pushed forward to the point where, eventually, Patterson would be indicted for murder in the first degree. It should have been a relatively simple case for the police and other officials. Two people were alone in a small and closed space. A weapon was fired once and one of those people died. There were no witnesses and nothing was heard from the cab except for the single shot, and that was heard only by the hansom driver. The question that remained was whether or not the sole living person who was in the hansom when the shot was fired had a felonious involvement in the death. It should have been easy; it was not.

Two accounts that appeared on June 5, one in a Richmond Virginia newspaper and one from a St. Paul Minnesota paper both featured Millin's remarks about Nan Patterson, all of which were highly negative. Yet no rebuttal was sought from people such as Nan's sister Julia (Mrs. J. Morgan Smith) or anybody else who might have been more neutral. Both mentioned Millin's remarks to Nan that she had killed his partner. But none of these accounts sought any information from the cab driver Michaels, except the comments noted above. By this time that coat and shirt of Young had been examined in the coroner's office and, said an account; "There was no trace of powder marks and no bullet hold in the coat pocket in which the pistol was found." The autopsy had also been performed by this time and it was said that the examining physician declared he was unable to say whether the wound was self-inflicted or not. Some of Young's friends, other than Millin, said the Europe trip had as its object the breaking off of his relationship with Nan. This was uncorroborated with independent witnesses and had the impact of inferring a motive to Nan to shoot Caesar, as the spurned mistress. Later evidence showed that Young was not keen to end the relationship, although various people around him, and not just Mrs. Young, were the anxious ones trying to sever the connection. One of these headlines declared, neutrally; "Caesar Young is killed in a cab," while the other bluntly asserted; "Murdered in a hansom."

While Millin had been in the police station where Nan was being questioned and held, and in the coroner's office [located in the same building] on June 4 and where he had screamed out his accusations against Nan he also tried, on at least two separate occasions, to physically attack Patterson. It had also been determined that the bullet that killed Young entered the body high up on the left side; it had a downward trajectory, passed through the left lung and lodged in the fourth vertebrae.

A St. Louis newspaper had more neutral subheads for its piece; "mysteriously shot to death," and "killed in cab with actress." Doctor O'Hanlon was the medical man who performed the autopsy and while the physician had said he was unable to say whether the wound was self-inflicted or not, this account declared it was "the sort of wound that a man would be unlikely to inflict on himself." Following that autopsy Coroner Brown, who had first set bail at $1,000, and than moved it to $5,000, decided to hold her without bail. According to this account Young came to the United States from England 13 years earlier, 1891, at the solicitation of some of the old Manhattan Athletic Club members at a time when track and field contests between various athletic clubs were popular events with the individual clubs striving mightily to best the rival clubs. Back then, in 1891, William Young was the most famous sprinter in England and it was to him that the invitation to come to America was extended. However, he was in Australia at the time and his young brother, Frank Young, came in his stead. Said a reporter; "He proved his mettle in many famous cross-county matches and all the while lived lavishly at the Manhattan clubhouse. When the club was in financial difficulties Young found himself in the street. He got work at $10 a week with the Western Union Telegraph Company as manager of messengers." He looked for a better position and found one with James Mahoney, "the poolroom king." Mahoney soon placed his new employee in charge of his uptown betting rooms when it became apparent to Mahoney that Young was good at establishing odds. Later, Young left the poolroom business and became a horse owner. A few years later he drifted west where he became wealthy, with the aid of his wife who handled all the family financial matters such as investments and buying real estate.

Another New York City newspaper observed that the police were "inclined to believe Young was murdered." This account noted that Patterson was well known in local theatrical circles and had been with two *Floradora* companies for some time. While she had only been with one *Floradora* company this account at least correctly the false reports that she had been with the original sextet with the original New York City company, which went on to achieve fame and to give birth to the various touring road companies that were set up in the wake of that success.

A lengthy piece with more detail appeared on June 5 in the *New York Tribune*. It noted that Nan met Caesar three years earlier in California, then later in Chicago and then came to New York with him five weeks previous. In this account there was no mention of any letters of a threatening nature written by Patterson and found on Young's body. Again, that was because no such letters existed. According to this report Young came to America in 1890 to represent the Manhattan Club in its bitter foot race rivalry with other institutions such as the New York Athletic Club and the Boston Athletic Club. It was in that period that Young got his sobriquet "Caesar," supposedly from the close resemblance of his profile to that of Julius Caesar. While he was said to have arrived in America without a cent, over the following 14 years he amassed a fortune of from $500,000 to $600,000, owned a ranch in Sacramento California, a horse breeding farm in Sacramento, real estate in New York City, and an interest in a race track. In 1890 when the Manhattan Athletic Club and the New York Athletic Club were locked in a fight for road race supremacy, representatives from the former went to England to recruit some of the famous athletes there. Finding William Young to be in Australia they settled for recruiting his brother Frank. He proved his worth winning many of the long distance and cross-country runs in which he was entered. But when the Manhattan Athletic Club folded Young found himself penniless. [While it fell into receivership and was dissolved in 1893 a new Manhattan Athletic Club emerged a year or so later]. During his time with the Manhattan Athletic Club Young met Margaret Becker, the daughter of well-to-do parents; she became Mrs. Young. From there he branched out into bookmaking and started to follow the racing circuit – going on to New Orleans. Soon thereafter he went on to California. Mrs. Young was said to have handled all the money and invested heavily in New York City apartment houses.

This account also featured more material from hansom driver Michaels, who verified that he was unaware of anything going on in his cab until he heard the shot. He explained that he picked up the couple at 8:00 AM with the destination being the pier; "Before I got there I heard a shot and pulled up. I did not hear a quarrel during any part of the drive. I heard the woman tell the policeman that the man said to her, before the shooting, that he was going away for some time, and might see her again or might not see her...Then, she said, a shot was fired. I also heard the woman tell the policeman that she and the dead man had been lovers for three years and it was a source of jealousy to

Mrs. Young." Readers were also informed that New York Police Department officer Junior was the first policeman on the scene and that he saw the man's body lying across the woman's lap; that he saw no gun, but later found one in the man's right hand coat pocket. Neither Michaels nor Junior saw anybody else anywhere near the site of the shooting; a fact conveniently ignored later when "witness" after "witness" after "witness" came forward to declare they had been onsite and had seen everything. In fact Michaels, the most likely candidate to have any knowledge of the event, was completely ignored by the press and, after this day, was not heard from again until he testified during the trials. When Nan spoke to Coroner Brown she also stated that Young had been despondent but that he had no money worries.

When the shot was fired Nan was sitting on the left side of the cab with Young beside her on the right. Powder marks and a bullet hole were evident in the shoulder of the coat and shirt. Following the various conversations Brown had he held a meeting with Assistant District Attorneys Appleton and Gans wherein it was declared that if the $5,000 bail that had been fixed by the Coroner should be offered they would take steps to have the amount raised so that Patterson would not be released. Nan, by then, had as lawyers Abraham Levy and Philip Waldheimer.

A different New York City newspaper, the *Sun*, told its readers that Margaret Young was said to have letters threatening her husband's life. This was a slight variation on previous accounts that those letters were found on Young's body. However, it was all nonsense as such letters did not exist, anywhere. Yet such false information was reported to have been the basis for an increase in Nan's bail. After Coroner Nicholas T. Brown heard the particulars of the case and "of the existence of certain letters" he caused her bail to be raised from $1,000 to $5,000, all based on the rumor of the existence of such letters. No one had actually seen them. That trip to Europe was said, herein, to last from several months up to a year. On the pier, awaiting the arrival of Caesar, were Margaret Young, Mrs. and Mrs. William

Luce and Young's business partner John D. Millin. While the Youngs were in New York they stayed at the home of Luce, who was a brother-in-law to Caesar. Mrs. Luce was a sister to Margaret. All of the couple's baggage, consisting of several trunks had been loaded aboard the White Star Line's Germanic and the best stateroom on the ship had been reserved. Sailing time was 9:30 AM.

Mrs. Smith, at the St. Paul Hotel, received the call from Caesar at 7:30 AM. He told her to tell Nan to meet him as quickly as possible. Nan, then in bed, got up, dressed quickly, and left the apartment. She met him just before 8:00AM. First stop was a saloon where Young had a whiskey. Then he had the cab stop while he went into a hat shop and bought a straw hat. Another stop was made at a bar for more drinks. When the cab, traveling about West Broadway, reached the intersection of Franklin Street Young told Patterson that they must part and that the separation might be for a few months or might be forever. Just after that remark, said Nan, she heard a muffled shot. In this account Nan met Young in California two to three years earlier and the pair quickly became intimate, at a time when Nan was with one of the western *Floradora* road companies. Soon Mrs. Young head abut the affair. Then Margaret heard a rumor, earlier in 1904, that Caesar and Patterson were about to elope. Millin and Mrs. Young watched the pair and tailed them to a railway station in Los Angeles one night and found the couple with their tickets already purchased and about to leave for Washington D.C. The elopement was stopped when Millin decked Caesar with his fist. Nan went east and continued writing to Caesar. In the meantime Young left San Francisco on April 5, with Margaret. They stopped at Chicago. Mrs. Young went on to New York City alone while Caesar stayed over in Chicago for a day, claiming he wanted to collect a debt. Young met Nan in Chicago and went on the Washington with her. This story is also not accurate but some elements of it were accurate; it was not wholly manufactured. A description of Patterson offered by this article went as follows; "She is merely an apple-faced colorless sort of person, with features which would be described as common...the general suggestion of her face is coarseness and heaviness...Her history is pretty much without interest." It was an odd description of a woman who, in other accounts of the time, was depicted as an evil, yet potent vamp, able to cause men [other than Young] to commit suicide after they had failed to capture and retain her charms.

An illustration that accompanied a June 5 article published in the San Francisco *Call* both smeared Patterson and was the first to come out with the idea that she would be charged with murder for it carried a headline stating that the "wrecker of the bookmaker's home will be charged with his murder." It was typical of the era that in such an "illicit" relationship as the one between Young and Patterson it was the female who was blamed for everything. It was just as accurate, and more sensible, to say that Young "wrecker" his home through his outside sexual activities. One earlier article implied that he had done so many times before Nan. In this piece it was said that Margaret Young "is a beautiful and talented woman..." That she knew of her husband's infatuation for Nan and it was to destroy that infatuation that she had persuaded him to go to Europe. With respect to that infatuation, wrote a journalist; "He seemed to be unable to withstand her blandishments...At times his infatuation became so intense that he was crazed. Twice he was taken care of by his friends until his wife could reach him. Mrs. Young seemed to have an influence upon him when she was with him that was even greater than that exerted by Nan Patterson. So it may be that he shot himself while temporarily insane, as a few of his friends believe." He was said to never have carried a gun, according to his friends and they wondered why he should do so at the start of a foreign trip. His wife looked after his clothing and she said he had no gun that Saturday morning when he left home. According to what little forensic examination had taken place no stains or powder marks were found on Nan's hands while stains (believed to be powder, pending tests to be made) were found on Young's hands.

A separate piece that appeared the same day in the *Call* continued the smear campaign against Patterson. The reporter asserted that both Nan and Young were well known in Los Angeles and that she appeared in that city about one year earlier and give it out that she was one of the members of the *Floradora* chorus but had tired on the stage. She was accompanied by a man whose name has been "forgotten" because she dropped him as soon as she saw richer pickings in the horsemen and racing crowd. Patterson then took up with Millin but quickly dropped him when she realized Young was the money man of the pair. Then she spent as much time as she could with Young and appeared to wield "amazing influence" over Caesar. He paid for her apartments, clothing, bought her expensive presents and so forth. Those of the sporting fraternity in Los Angeles who knew both people, said the journalist; "blame her for Young's downfall..." That downfall involved excessive drinking, neglecting his business and so forth. When Young went north to San Francisco Nan went also and she could "seemingly dominate" Young. Friends of Caesar refrained from offering him advice, with respect to his mistress, because they feared his displeasure. None of this material about Patterson was credited to anybody, not even the usual and ubiquitous "anonymous source." Young was a massive drinker before he met Patterson. The caricature sketches of the 13 well-known San Francisco track men mentioned earlier shows Caesar, almost 18 months before his death with what could clearly be interpreted as a red drinker's nose.

The main players in the tragedy. Mrs. Frank Thomas Young (middle). Note the headline portraying Nan as a "home-wrecker" while Caesar could have justifiably been so labeled. Not also Nan's name is given as Mrs. Patterson, even though she had been divorced for a year. And when she was married her name was Mrs. Martin

CHAPTER 2.
INVESTIGATION AND INDICTMENT.

From the third day after the tragedy (Monday, June 6) until the tenth day (Monday, June 13) the investigation continued and culminated in the indictment of Ann Elizabeth Patterson for murder in the first degree. In was during this period that various lying attention-seekers began to pop up, "witnesses" who had seen it all. Sadly, the media gave their stories much coverage and treated it all seriously. More and more time was spent trying to trace the gun and determine how it arrived in the hansom cab that morning. Nan continued to be smeared in the press while her legal team began to make motions to have her released on bail; none would ever prove to be successful.

On that Monday, June 6, proceedings began by Coroner Nicholas Brown in an attempt to solve the mystery of Young's death. Reportedly six New York Police Department detectives were working on the gun issue alone. And for the first time the wider background of Patterson and her family started to be explored. She was a Washington D. C. women who had spent most of her life there, although she was not born in the nation's capital. Her father was John Randolph Patterson and was said to be "well known in the real estate circles of Washington. Her father had already been in New York to visit his daughter in custody but the Patterson family was then not willing to discuss the case. One of these articles had as its title, "Mrs. Nan Patterson."

Mrs. and Mrs. John Randolph Patterson of 1911 14th Street

northwest were reported to be "prostrated" with grief at their home. Herein it was said that the father went to New York City to see his daughter, on Sunday night, June 5. Also living at home was Charles W. Patterson, about 21 years old and employed as a clerk in a haberdasher's store on Fourteenth Street. John Patterson was for many years, reportedly, the Supervising Architect of the Treasury. He resigned from that post at the time of Grover Cleveland's election victory to the position of United States President (elected in 1884 and installed in March 1885). Patterson, a Republican, resigned because he refused to hold office under a Democrat. In recent years he had been devoting himself to the real estate business. Nan was the great-granddaughter of John Randolph of Roanoke, a man who had served various terms in the US House of Representatives, a term in the US Senate, as well as being Minister to Russia in 1830. When Nan took the stage name of Randolph it was this relative she named herself after. One of her uncles, Charles P, Patterson was the cashier of the Fourth National Bank of New York and still another uncle was a US Senator from New Hampshire. Nan Patterson was born in 1882 and attended the Barrett School. She met a New York man named Leon Gaines Martin when she was a teenager and married him when she was just 16 years old. They lived together for only about one year; Martin then being employed by a San Francisco railroad. While in San Francisco Nan became fascinated by the stage. Martin alleged that one reason why he got a divorce was because his wife became "inordinately fond of dress" and he could not afford to give her the luxuries she wanted. In 1901 she joined a *Floradora* company, but only had a minor part. For the first time it was revealed that Caesar and Nan had spent some time together, on at least two occasions on Friday, June 3. Other people were with each of them on those occasions. One thing that was clear from that information was that Patterson knew abut the Europe trip and possible separation prior to Saturday, June 4.

A separate article from a Washington D. C. newspaper told its readers that Leon Martin and Nan grew up together on the same street and the pair knew each other from age six. The problem with that story was that Martin was about 14 years older than Patterson. Martin told a reporter they had parted three years earlier; "I can't believe that the girl shot the man, for, although she is a strange emotional creature, she is not vicious, and she always was extremely afraid of firearms." Added Martin; "Nan is lively and loves pleasure. We were married only a year when we decided we could not get along together. She had the stage fever...My wife was inordinately fond of dress, and I could not afford to get her the luxuries she craved...I have not seen her for two years. I had never heard of this man Young."

One of the very few people contacted by the press who did not have an ax to grind against Nan was a woman named Helen Morrison. She was a member of that same *Floradora* company that introduced Patterson to the public. Morrison traveled with her through the West, chummed around with her and roomed with Nan. Morrison said her friend never had a gun; "She was too timid to own such a thing. I never knew a girl who was quite so timid. She was almost helpless...She could be easily influenced as readily to do wrong as to do right. One needed merely to call and Nan would obey." Added Morrison; "I see Mr. Young's partner says she caused three men to commit suicide. That is absurd. He says she caused a member of the *Ben Hur* company to shoot himself." She explained that he had confused the show with the *Floradora* company. William Herr, manager of their company was nicknamed Ben Hur. He became infatuated with Nan. He was separated at the time and very attentive to Nan until she met Young. "I have known Nan very well and I am quite sure the only affairs she had have been those with Herr and Young," continued Morrison. Helen also observed that Young was the one who chased after Patterson. He sought her out, not the other way around.

It was admitted on that Monday, June 6, that on the previous day Patterson had visits to the jail from her sister Julia (Mrs. J. Morgan Smith), her father, and her lawyer. Sometime on that day she was allowed a change of clothing. Only later would the problem be noted that the clothing she wore on that fateful morning was never subjected to any forensic examination for powder burns, and so forth. By the time the issue was raised no one knew where the clothing had gone, or even who had provided the change of clothing. But it was a problem generated by the state. One later explanation provided was that initial forensic examination had been minimal because at first the case was regarded as a suicide. Such errors by the state began to loom large because, as one reporter put it that day, "reasons multiply for why it was not suicide." The first strange and/or bizarre appearance in what would become a long line of "witnesses" surfaced in the person of an unnamed witness who had been found who claimed he had once seen such a weapon, as the gun used in the shooting, in the possession of Nan's brother-in-law J. Morgan Smith. The subject of "letters" was again raised but this account admitted that it was not clear if they existed or if anyone had actually seen them, and that while no one had actually seen them the reporter was confident enough to declare there were "not of a threatening nature." Also noted was that Young made no attempt to conceal his love for his mistress yet he was supposedly determined to break the affair off. Caesar's brother-in-law William Luce met Nan on the Friday night before the shooting for a couple of hours to talk about the coming separation. Luce declared she told him she would go to the pier the following morning and "make trouble for him". Young was with Luce during that time and Luce said that Young placated her by saying if she would be good he would call her in the morning and would let her ride downtown with him. Later it was revealed that it was John Millin who said Nan's brother-in-law Smith had a pistol like the one fund in the cab. Also reported herein was that professional boxer Young Corbett II (William J. Rothwell), World Featherweight Champion 1901-1902, had his manager offer to post bail for Nan on the Saturday. That offer from a man described as an "ardent admirer" of Patterson was refused by the state.

Lawyers Henry W. Unger and Daniel O'Reilly secured a writ

of habeas corpus for Patterson from Justice Clarke in the New York State Supreme Court on the morning of June 6; it commanded the warden of the Tombs to produce her before the court at 10:30 AM on the following day. What was supposedly new evidence led to the postponement of the inquest into the Young death, also that day. William Luce came forward to assert that Young said to him on Friday night June 3rd; "I want you to come along in case anything happens [when I see Nan later tonight]. She has most valuable letters of mine and I must get them." He did not get them and that accounted for the Saturday morning meeting before the ship sailed, or at least that was what Luce declared. It was all a lie. Other new evidence came from a B. S. McKean, another brother-in-law of Young (married to another of Young's sisters). His deposition related a number of supposed times when, he said, Patterson threatened Young. A description of Nan when she was in the coroner's office said; "The woman's attire was so plain that it looked as though she had deliberately made herself as unattractive as possible...The girl is far from handsome..." This account repeated the false idea that Young agreed to meet her on the Saturday morning to prevent her making a scene at the pier. No meeting had ever been arranged on that Friday night. On Saturday morning Patterson was asleep and probably would have slept through sailing time but for Young's phone call (later shown to be several) which was spontaneous and got his mistress out of bed.

An account in a different newspaper reported the supposed conversation Young had with Luce on the Friday night when the former asked his relative to accompany him to the meeting with Nan that night. According to this piece Young said; "The little woman has some letters which I must get from her. I'm afraid of her, and I don't know but what she might kill me. I'm through with her. I intend to break it off to-night." Meanwhile, Frank Thomas Young was buried on June 7 and the police had reportedly come up with a new theory about Young's demise. In this scenario Nan attempted suicide because Young was about to leave her and in the struggle for possession of the pistol as Caesar, presumably tried to stop his mistress, he was accidentally killed.

A few days after the shooting it was reported that New York Police Department detectives had traced the ownership of the revolver from the manufacturer to the retailer, and were hopeful of determining ownership of the weapon. The revolver used to kill Young was said to have come from the retail establishment of Schoverling, Daly and Gales, at 302 Broadway, San Francisco. More dubious "information" came to light in this piece when it was noted that Nan was to have sailed for Europe early in May 1904 and that passage for her was engaged and paid for for Caesar but at the last moment she refused to go unless he would go with her. When Nan learned that Young and his wife intended to said for Europe, Nan was prepared to follow them. It was even said in this piece that she even went so far as to arrange for passage on one of the liners sailing from New York on June 7. This theory was so bizarre and fanciful that no other newspapers seem to have published it. Most of the false information was picked up by other newspapers and printed because they were all at the mercy of the material on the wire services and/or the onsite reporters from the very large dailies, such as in New York City and Washington. A description of Nan's father, John Randolph Patterson went as follows; "the aged and decrepit father" and stated she had been "estranged" from her parents but when her present troubles arose her "old father" forgot the differences from the past and prepared to spend his last dollar to defend his daughter. [He was 68 years old]. No source was given for that "estrangement" idea but it added to that idea that Nan was somehow evil, morally bankrupt, and so forth. For a final touch the journalist said that "Nan Patterson had other admirers than Caesar Young..."

Later reports corrected the listing of the sporting goods retailer (including handguns) to be Schoverling, Daly and Gales, located at 302 Broadway, New York City. The maker of the revolver was said to be based in Springfield Massachusetts, but not named [perhaps Smith & Wesson]. It was also noted that Nan's hands were not examined [for powder residue] until four or five hours had elapsed after the shooting and that her clothing "was not examined with any care." Hours also elapsed before the hands of the dead man were examined for powder residue.

Nan's brother Charles W. Patterson spoke to the press briefly on June 7, from the family home in Washington D. C. He said that Nan was always on good terms with the family and she visited the family home in the nation's capital every month or so. According to the brother Nan ran away from school at the age of 16, to Baltimore with Leon Martin, where they were married. He claimed she was devoted to Martin but that he deserted her and then she went on the stage to support herself. She did not let the family know of that development at the time but later on, after obtaining a position on the stage, she wrote to the family about her new circumstances, and came to Washington for a visit. Nan's father John had been a resident of New Hampshire but moved to Washington early in life and all of his children were born in Washington. His wife came from a state of Virginia background.

On June 7 Nan was back in court when she appeared before Justice Clarke, on habeas corpus proceedings. Henry W. Unger, one of her lawyers, contended that as Nan had not been charged with any crime her commitment was plainly illegal. The courtroom was reportedly jammed "with the curious." Daniel O'Reilly, another of her lawyers was also in the courtroom during those proceedings and, observed a reporter; "After leaving the court in the morning Mr. O'Reilly was obliged to use his cane as a club to open a path for his client through the mob that thronged the corridors." At the end of the day Clarke reserved his decision, denied her bail, and sent her back to the Tombs. Boxer Young Corbett was mentioned again and it was said that he went so far as to cancel at the last minute a trip to San Francisco to be on hand for the proceedings. Said Corbett; The girl is innocent. She never killed Young. She wouldn't harm a fly...I am convinced that she is getting the worst of it, and I am going to stand by her." Reportedly, he had involved himself in getting counsel for her and had declared himself ready to post bail for Nan, yet he said he did not know her and had only spoken to her once or twice at a meeting. In a separate development J. Morgan Smith was picked up on a warrant and taken to the office of Assistant District Attorney Garvan where he was questioned by New York Police Department detectives and by Garvan. Specifically he was asked about ownership of the gun involved in the shooting and of his whereabouts at the time of the shooting. Smith refused to answer any questions and was eventually released. Smith and his wife Julia (Nan's sister) were to play an increasingly larger role as time passed, in one of the more bizarre aspects of the case.

As of June 7 the following four men were listed as lawyers for Patterson; Daniel O'Reilly, Abraham Levy, Henry W. Unger and Philip Waldheimer. O'Reilly was said to have been retained by Nan's father John Patterson. Garvan had asked that the inquest into Young's death be postponed, in light of new evidence, and it was postponed for at least several days. That new evidence was the aforementioned letters that William Luce spoke of in his affidavit. In other developments, it had been confirmed by Florence Black, telephone operator [in a latter account in chapter 5 she was named as Ida F. Townsend] at the St. Paul Hotel, that Caesar Young had called Nan on the Saturday morning of his death. During those early days of the telephone industry all calls, including local ones, had to go through a live operator. Also determined was that the gun was manufactured in 1898, that it was a five-shot revolver and that when the police recovered it the weapon had one empty chamber, three chambers were loaded and the remaining chamber held a discharged cartridge. A quantity of powder of Young's right hand had still not been identified as lab tests were still pending. This account speculated that while on the surface O'Reilly had been hired by Nan's father the actual person involved was a "well known member of the sporting fraternity." Although not named, that individual was clearly Young Corbett. Meanwhile the Smiths, and everybody on Young's side all swore none had ever owner a revolver, or carried one. Nan continued to be held in the Tombs without charge, detained as a witness. Nominally she was held in lieu of $5,000 bail but in fact the state had no intention of releasing her even if someone came forward willing to post that amount. In the end, no one did come forward to make a firm offer to post bail. And on that day, June 8, another new twist was added; the first of the attention-seeking "eye-witnesses" stepped forward. Algernon Meyer of Jacksonville Florida announced publicly that he was a witness to the death of Young and explained that Young himself held the revolver that fired the fatal shot He told his story first to a newspaper and then went to the District Attorney's office and told them he had decided to make a formal statement. According to Meyer, who said he witnessed the scene the shooting appeared to be accidental. Nan was struggling with Young who had the revolver in his right hand and his right arm was around her neck. Meyer also said there was another witness to the shooting, besides himself. It was a man in a dark suit, wearing a straw hat and who had a small black mustache. According to the story told by Meyer he was walking on West Broadway on that Saturday morning when his attention was drawn to a cab coming down the street. As he looked the occupants – a man and a woman – began to scuffle. At that point, during their scuffle, right in front of him, the other man approached, stopped and observed the scene. Then a shot was fired. The cab didn't stop. That was just before the cab passed Meyer and just as the other man had run out into the street and jumped up on the cab step.

Not surprisingly the story about Meyer drew a lot of press coverage. The New York City paper the *World* claimed that it interviewed him. Algernon C. Meyer of Jacksonville Florida was said to be a solicitor for the Bureau of National Literature and Art, which had an office in Washington D. C. Meyer had come north for business reasons. When he was asked the obvious question as to why he had not stayed at the scene and given a statement then to the police, all he told the reporter was' "I had a reason for not wanting to be mixed up in the affair, but when I bought the newspapers Saturday afternoon and saw the case looked bad for the woman, I determined to speak if it became necessary." He added that he had never heard the names Caesar Young or Nan Patterson in his life. In relating his story to the *World*, Meyer gave as a reference to his character the National Bank of Jacksonville. A telegram from that bank, in response to a request for information from the newspaper, stated; "So far as we can learn Meyer's reputation for truth and veracity is good." Meyer also explained to the newspaper that he told his aunt, Genevieve Grimme of New York City, the story on Saturday afternoon, before he read the newspapers. When approached by the reporter Grimme agreed that Meyer had told her the story but added; "In our family we have always regarded Algie as a youth with a vivid imagination and I did not pay much attention to him." Grimme told her nephew, anyway, to keep out of the whole business. Supposedly, Meyer also told his story to Arthur O. Gandy in New York City, a broker who handled an account for Algernon. The reporter then showed the story to Nan's lawyers, Unger and O'Reilly and asked for comment. Said Unger; "He is one of dozens. We have received stacks of letters every day from people who said they saw the shooting. Some said that they saw Young shoot the woman and others that they saw the woman shoot Young. Most of the letters were not signed."

But, of course, the "eye-witnesses" did not stop with Meyer. Lawyer Unger said he had an important witness in Henry A. Katz, an insurance agent. Unger had been informed, he stated, that Katz was a witness to the shooting of Young and was prepared to testify that it was a case of suicide. Not to be outdone in the witness sweepstakes, the office of District Attorney Jerome came forward to announce that they had found another witness in the shape of Carl Norlander. Supposedly, he may, or may not have been the pedestrian who leaped upon the step of the cab just after the shooting. That is, he may have been the man described by Meyer, the guy with the straw hat and mustache. All of these "eye-witnesses" were lying; there was no element of truth in what they were saying.

J. Morgan Smith found himself dragged deeper and deeper into the morass. A report emerged that claimed the revolver used in the shooting had been sold by a Schoverling employee named G. R. Schneider in November 1898, although that clerk had no idea to whom he had sold the weapon. A helpful hint was supplied to the reader when the article observed that J. Morgan was in New York city during the summer, fall and early winter of 1898. While Smith had refused to answer questions when he was first grilled by the authorities he then found himself the recipient of a subpoena that directed him to appear on the morning of June 8 before the Grand Jury. All records at that gun store in New York City had been destroyed in a fire. The weapon arrived at the Schoverling outlet some five years earlier and the fire had occurred soon after that. A separate set of records, not lost in the fire revealed the name of the clerk who sold the gun, but nothing else was containing in that record. Presumably, the records destroyed in the fire contained more complete records, including the name of the buyer. In the wake of Caesar's funeral it was noted that Mrs. Young was confined to her bed and had refused to eat since the Saturday shooting [it was then Wednesday] and; "It is feared that she may die from weakness and shock, or else go mad. She has hysterical crying spells.." That, of course, was nonsense. Similar reports about Nan would surface from time to time, about her hysteric reactions to one thing or another, and so forth. Around that same time it was reported that Nan had no eaten for three days. Throughout the period of Nan's incarceration it was regularly noted, from time to time, that Mrs. Patterson (Nan's mother) was seriously ill, lying prostrate, at death's door, and so on, all because of the case. Such reports about women and their reactions to things were a regular feature of the news. All played into the patriarchy's narrative about weak, irrational, hysterical and generally useless women, unable to cope with anything and forever overreacting emotionally. And, could not such a woman go mad at any moment and crazily and irrationally shoot somebody?

Most of the slanders against Nan had at least a passing relationship to the case, but not all. It was reported that police were investigating reports of an episode in a Seventh Avenue Hotel in New York City, from "a short time ago." According to information possessed by the police Nan, while "hysterical," displayed a knife, which it was said, was taken away from her with difficulty after a struggle; "She was much excited and it is said that threats were made which the police regard as having a bearing upon the present case."

On June 9 the Grand Jury had under investigation the case of Nan Patterson. Three witnesses were brought into the case. One of them was taken to the Tombs jail and permitted to see Patterson as she sat in her cell. That was done for the purpose of identifying her, if possible, as the person who purchased the revolver used in the shooting. Assistant District Attorney Garvan would not identify the witness nor let him talk to anybody Later Garvan claimed the witness to be H. A. Katz of 20 West 12th Street. However, a reporter determined that address would be Mount Morris Park. More mention was made herein about Meyer and that the police; "became convinced that his story will not stand a severe investigation," after they took him physically over the scene of the tragedy. Unger was reported to be more inclined to doubt Meyer's story than was the District Attorney's office. In this account it was said that Meyer had first contacted Unger with his tale. The shot was fired when the cab was in or around the intersection of West Broadway and Franklin Street. However, Meyer placed it at the intersection of West Broadway and Walker Street, two blocks away.

When he dismissed the writ of habeas corpus filed on Nan's behalf, Justice John Proctor Clarke said the paperwork filed with the proceedings disclosed to him abundant justification for holding her. While Nan was then prepared to furnish bail officials refused to accept any bail, although it remained set at a nominal $5,000. Had Nan been released by Clarke on the writ of habeas corpus she would have been immediately arrested on a charge of murder in the first degree. Judge Olmstead, of Special Sessions Court, had issued that arrest warrant and detectives were waiting at the Tombs to arrest her as soon as she appeared, in case bail was posted, and accepted by the state. Rumors circulated that the mystery witness who was brought to Nan's cell in the hopes of identifying the prisoner, perhaps named Katz, was a pawnbroker who had sold her the weapon. Note that nothing like a lineup was involved.

In spite of pleas from District Attorney William T. Jerome the Grand Jury, on the afternoon of June 9, refused to indict Patterson for the murder of Young, without first hearing the girl's story from her own lips. To that end the Grand Jury issued an invitation to Nan to appear before them. Her lawyer declined that invitation on her behalf on the ground that it was improper to call an accused person before that body. That mystery identifier was finally correctly identified as a pawnbroker named Hyman Stern, who conducted his business at 516 Sixth Avenue, New York City. However, after viewing Nan in her cell he was unable to identify her as the person who visited his place at the time the pistol was bought. Stern was instructed to remain at police headquarters until Mr. and Mrs. J. Morgan Smith could be brought before him to see if he could identify one or the other of them as the buyer of the weapon. Mr. Smith, however, could not be found. Yet another baseless slander against Patterson found its way into print in this article. Reportedly, police had learned that Nan held up Young with a pistol and attempt to shoot him in the Imperial Hotel about two weeks earlier. That story was said to have come from Young's relatives, who alleged that Caesar told them of the event. Neither the "facts" from this baseless nonsense nor the one mentioned earlier ever made it into court testimony in any of Nan's three trials.

Another bizarre "eye-witness" surfaced on June 9. It was claimed that this man's story corroborated the tale told by Meyer. The new man was Louis Katzenburg, a salesman with the Knickerbocker Suspender Company. Katzenburg said he saw the cab with the man who had jumped onto the step. He did not see the shooting or hear the gunshot but his attention was drawn by the man on the cab's step. And he claimed to have seen that man just below Walker Street. He explained that when he read of the shooting in the newspaper he knew that was the cab he saw. And, remarked a journalist both Katzenburg and Meyer had the "best of business reasons" for not wanting their names to be publicly tied to the case. However, the reader was never to be informed just what those reasons might have been. And there was still another new man. This newly found man was named William Haskins who said he heard the pistol shot but saw nothing. He also placed the event at Walker Street and not Franklin Street and thus backed up the nonsense spouted by Meyer and Katzenburg.

Police were trying to find J. Morgan Smith on June 10, in order to serve a summons on him requiring him to appear before the Grand Jury and tell what he might know about the case. Reportedly Smith and his wife left their apartment at the St. Paul Hotel in New York City on Wednesday June 8 and their current whereabouts were unknown. Stern, the pawnbroker who allegedly sold the revolver found in Young's pocket said he was positive he could identify the weapon and the man and woman to whom he sold it. Besides being taken physically to see Nan in the cell he had been shown a photograph of Patterson. However, he could not identify her as the female half of the couple whom he said had purchased the gun.

Another dramatic scene unfolded near the coroner's office when Nan was being led back to the Tombs. Mrs. William Luce, sister of the dead man, confronted Nan and cried out; "You fiend, you did it." She tried to get close enough to make physical contact with Patterson but was prevented from doing so by police officers and was led away.

Another hit piece on Patterson appeared in a Salt Lake City Utah newspaper around this time. It purported to outline what had happened in that city when Nan visited there, as a member of the *Floradora* company, in the fall of 1902. According to the reporter; "At the time although she was reputed to have a score of suitors in her train, she was believed to be affianced to Tommy Burns, the jockey. This, however, did not deter her from breaking hearts when the opportunity presented itself. In Salt Lake her conquest was as easy as it has been elsewhere. Her affairs in the east were merely 'affairs.' The west presented a new field." She was described as being fond of late wine suppers, cards and dice; she also gambled a little. She had an affair with a well known and well to do young man of Salt Lake City but they parted when she left for the west coast. Three days later in San Francisco, she met and made "an easy victim" of Caesar Young. Herein it was said that affair was broken up briefly by Mr. Young but she had again joined Young in 1903 in San Francisco, when she was no longer on stage. This account was likely completely fabricated; no sources of any kind, not even the ubiquitous and unhelpful anonymous ones, were given.

The Smiths hit the news again when, on June 10, it was announced that the coroner's inquest into the death of Young was halted again, this time because of the disappearance of the couple. Pawnbroker Stern alleged he sold the revolver to a man and a woman in his shop on the day before the shooting, which was Friday, June 3. On Tuesday June 7 J. Morgan Smith was questioned by Garvan of the District Attorney's office but refused to answer any questions. He was released but then Smith was served with a subpoena to appear before the Grand Jury on Wednesday June 8. He did appear and spent several hours at the criminal courts building that day but the case was not presented to the Grand Jury and Smith, along with the other witnesses on hand, all went home. Then, after that, pawnbroker Stern surfaced and told his story, later on the Wednesday. Reportedly, the Smith couple packed up their belongings and left their apartment on that Wednesday evening. According to Stern's story, on Friday a man and a woman entered his store at 516 Sixth Avenue and asked to look at some revolvers. Among them was one of the type that Young was shot with. Stern knew it was indeed that weapon used because he made a note of the serial number when he sold it. The next task for Stern was to identify the couple that made that purchase. He was taken to view Nan in person – twice, although no lineup was involved – but could not name her as one member of the couple. Supposedly Young was at the races on that Friday afternoon and in other ways had an alibi, supposedly making it unlikely he had time to purchase the weapon. Later, Stern would be shown a photograph of Caesar; the pawnbroker could not identify him. Left unsaid specifically, but obviously implied, was the idea that the Smiths had fled the area because they feared being identified by Stern.

A different report of the disappearance of the Smiths observed that the couple were still guests of the St. Paul Hotel where they had been staying in New York City – that is, they had not formally checked out – but had not been seen there for four days. Their bills were all paid up to date and their luggage was still in their rooms. Following instructions from the authorities, Stern was not talking to the press. Still another "witness" lurched out of the woodwork. Counsel for Patterson received a letter from a man who signed himself Otto Mayer of 160 Bleecker Street, New York City. He claimed that he had been on West Broadway at the time of the shooting and Young and his companion in the cab and that Young drew a revolver and shot himself, despite the efforts of "Mrs. Patterson" to prevent him. An obvious question was why the press printed such nonsense from a seemingly endless parade of nut cases muttering nonsense. None of the stories they told, to that point, benefited the prosecution at all and the defense knew they were all baseless and ignored them. So why did the media devote as much space as they did to the tall tales? Perhaps it was just to have something different and unusual to write about in the case. Such cases tended to lag as days went by and little or nothing new seemed to happen. So perhaps such material allowed the newspapers to sensationalize, and, of course, to sell more papers.

Drawing the link between the Smiths and the weapon more

obviously was another reporter who declared that Stern "gave a complete description of J. Morgan Smith..." Stern had, by then, seen a photograph of Young and said definitely that it was not him. Admitting that the pawnbroker could not identify Nan, after two attempts, the journalist remarked; "But when he described the man who made the purchase it became apparent that he was referring to J. Morgan Smith, or a person greatly like him."

The appearance of so much nonsense in the press with respect to the "eye-witnesses" who came forward got so pervasive as to draw comment. Wrote a journalist; "The district attorney and the attorneys for Mrs. Patterson are much annoyed by the many stories brought forward by alleged eye-witnesses to the shooting. One of these persons brought forward a new account today, alleging that Young was shot by a man who jumped to the step of the cab in which Young and Mrs. Patterson were sitting and fired at Young over Mrs. Patterson's shoulder, but this statement received little credence." [This was a different man than the one Meyer alleged earlier who had jumped on the cab step]. When the Grand Jury had failed to indict Nan District Attorney Jerome said; "I do not believe the grand jury has refused to render an indictment in this case. In fact I know it had not. I attribute the fact of not filing an indictment to some error in presenting the indictment to the foreman of the grand jury for his signature, which makes the paper a true bill."

On June 11 counsel for Nan was said to have informed the District Attorney's office and also the police that J. Morgan Smith would be surrendering himself to the authorities on Monday June 13. Smith then had a contempt of court charge filed against him, for failing to appear before the Grand Jury, on the day after he had been sent home when the case was not called. A reporter speculated that Smith was then outside of New York State.

With respect to the disappearance of J. Morgan Smith one of Patterson's lawyers, Abraham Levy, stated; "He is doing Miss Patterson a great wrong by his conduct and I am amazed that the man should pursue such a coarse. He had nothing whatever to fear, and I shall do all in my power to discover his whereabouts and bring him forward." And with regard to the "silly season witnesses," Levy said; "The long-sought witness who was seen by several to jump up on the step of the hansom cab immediately after the shooting and whose presence was formally requested by Mr. William H. Rand Jr. [of the District Attorney's office] in an appeal sent out through the newspapers, proved to be as unimportant as have nearly all of the many 'eye witnesses' who have come forward during the past few days."

Smith was the son of Reverend J. Morgan Smith who, in his lifetime was, said a journalist, "a noted preacher with a reputation extending all over the United States. Dr. Smith was stationed at Grand Rapids Michigan, and there are scores of old residents of Grand Rapids scattered around the country who would go to any lengths to shelter his son." The Reverend Smith died in 1883, aged 50. A little more information about his son appeared in print in 1899 when it was reported that his son shipped from San Francisco as a common sailor on a whaling vessel for a two-year voyage. J. Morgan Smith was reported herein to be a cousin of plutocrat J. Pierpont Morgan of New York and in the previous six years was credited with having "squandered" $300,000. He was said to have been around the world several times and was a "society favorite."

New York Police Department Captain Sweeney advanced a theory on the case on June 11. He explained; "I think that Young shot himself accidentally as he was trying to get from the woman the revolver which she had drawn with the idea of committing suicide. That means, of course, that she did not kill him, and that she was innocent of any intention of killing him." Herein Nan was portrayed as a "cheerful" prisoner and that she "takes great pleasure in comforting her female companions." Then the article presented Nan's life story as told to the reporter, supposedly, by Helen Morrison "the best friend of the actress." They roomed together for almost a year when they were both members of the western *Floradora* road company. Nan was described as being about 21, born in Washington D. C., and having parents who were refined and fairly wealthy. She went to a private school in Washington, taking a special course in music. She married Martin at age 16 but soon separated and, added Morrison; "I know that it was not the girl's fault." Then she decided to go on stage. She made application for an engagement to John Fisher of the firm Fisher and Ryley, the managers of *Floradora*. She was hired "immediately." She then met Helen, who found her to be very timid. They opened in the stage production in Hartford Connecticut and, Helen explained, Nan always waited around in the theatre for an extra amount of time after the production ended, in hopes that the "stage-door johnnies" would be gone when she finally left the building. A month later they were in Salt Lake City. When the troupe reached San Francisco, a racehorse man with "lots of money" began to entertain the entire sextet. It was in that city that she began receiving attentions from a member of the company. Nan soon recognized it as a mistake and ended it. Patterson remained with the company until it closed in the east and then returned to California. It was then that she met Caesar Young. Morrison viewed her friend as a loving, clinging girl, incapable of murder.

 On Monday June 13 Ann Elizabeth Patterson was formally indicted for murder in the first degree. Concluding on that same day was the coroner's inquest which ended with a verdict that death came to Frank Thomas Young by a bullet wound. That indictment had been found on Friday June 10 but not signed until June 13. As soon as the indictment was handed down Assistant District Attorney Rand went into Coroner Brown's court (where the inquest was ongoing) to announce the indictment. Nan was present there and that was when she received the notice of the indictment. Lawyer Abraham Levy came forward at this time to declare that Smith would not return to New York City for a month or so. Reportedly he was then in Virginia, not far from Washington.

 A different account declared that Patterson broke down when she learned she had been indicted, and that she had been told of that fact by one of her lawyers. She was described herein as follows; "Mrs. Patterson is a medium-sized, brown-haired, blue-eyed siren of 24, loving and lovable in her mercurial way and the heroine of more than one 'affair.'" And the description continued; "She possesses a handsome, well-turned figure and affects the style of all *Floradora* girls. Like all women of her class, she is a hail-fellow-well-met, lavish with her money when she has any, given to 'good times,' but always with a cheery spirit." She met Caesar two years earlier "and although she had a number of 'affairs' on at the time, one being with Tommy Burns the jockey. Young became her favorite. He spent money on her lavishly and became extremely jealous of other men's attention to her. The woman's control over Young grew to such an extent that, despite his many efforts to break with her, he could not resist her influence." He capped it all by taking her to Los Angeles early in 1903, leaving his wife "to agonize." Mentioned was boxer Young Corbett as one of the "moths" who were "singed" by Patterson "as also were those of a prominent theatrical man and a wealthy lumberman from Oregon."

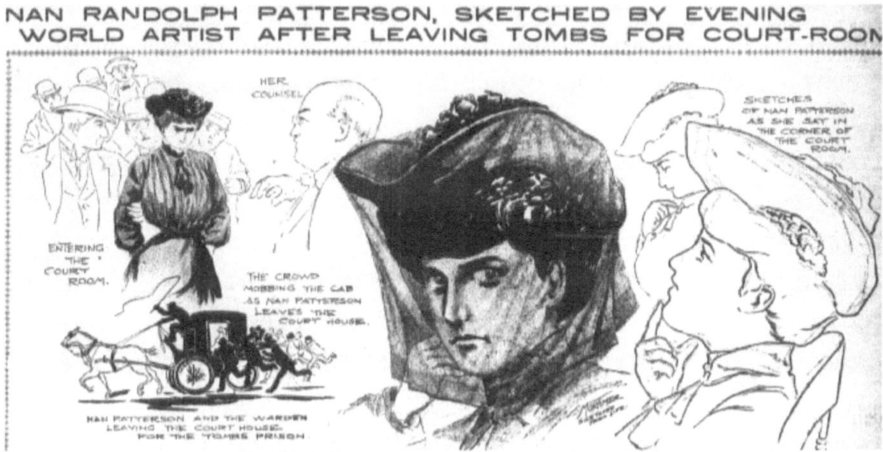

Sketches of Nan made by a New York City newspaper's illustrator depicting Patterson as she proceeded to and from court during the habeas corpus proceedings.

CHAPTER 3. FROM INDICTMENT TO TRIAL #1.

On Tuesday June 14 "Mrs Nan Patterson" appeared in court before Judge Newburger in the General Sessions Court where she entered a plea of not guilty. She came into court accompanied by her father, Martha McLaughlin (a friend whom she used to go to school with), and her counsel. The appearance was very brief and then she was quickly taken back to the Tombs. At that point the case was not expected to come to trial until the fall and therefore Nan would have to spend the summer in the Tombs. Most accounts declared that Nan in court "had collapsed under the strain, so that she had to have medical treatment." While the majority of accounts used some such language some added that she needed stimulants in court from a doctor to recover sufficiently enough to be escorted back to her cell. The New York County District Attorney, from 1902 to 1909, was William Travers Jerome. While he was in overall charge of the prosecution and persecution of Nan that was to follow and last for eleven straight months, most of the courtroom work was conducted by various Assistant District Attorneys, principally by Assistant District Attorney William Rand. Some of the decisions made and approved by Jerome, especially later in the case evidenced a cruel, and vicious nature on the part of the obviously misogynistic Jerome.

On the day of her court appearance to plead not guilty one journalist remarked that Nan was not the same woman as she was back on June 4. "That was a girl with a fresh, blooming face and bright eyes, a jaunty, self-possessed girl, sure of her looks and her ability to look after herself. It was a jaded drooping woman who stood before the bar of justice...Since her arrest Nan Patterson has aged ten years. Her face is sallow and her eyes are sunken. Her hair hangs in straggling bunches and her white hands are thin," observed the reporter. He added; "Her appetite has left her...The nervous strain to which she has been subjected has lead to a physical breakdown."

One of the smear articles noted, about Nan's life in the Tombs; "The Patterson girl has a hospital cell in which there is plenty of light and ventilation. She is visited by a Negro maid, who attends to dressing her hair and taking care of her clothing. Most of her time is spent in reading. Not a line that is printed about her case escapes her." And, not a line in this paragraph had any truth in it. It was all manufactured lies, presumably to smear the detainee, and to titillate the readers. What was true was that her father, John Randolph Patterson faithfully paid daily visits to the Tombs to be with his daughter, while Martha McLaughlin also visited regularly. Other than those two and her attorneys Nan would see and talk to no one else. Reportedly, since the indictment was announced; "She has eaten little since Monday, when wearied and ill she was led to her cell, and she also sleeps very little."

For the first time editorials about the case were published. One appeared in a Georgia newspaper wherein the editor declared there were three possibilities in the case: Young committee suicide; Nan's attempt at suicide led to Young's accidental death; and Patterson shot him. As far as the editor was concern there was no reason to suspect Young killed himself and he could see no reason why Nan would have tried to kill herself in the cab. While he drew no conclusion he had clearly left only one option remaining. Admitting that it was all still a mystery he thought that owing to that mystery the case would attract "wide attention."

On the same day an editorial appeared in the northwest part

of the country, in a Washington State newspaper that was more openly hostile. It mentioned that Nan was on stage for a "number of seasons" and "it is quietly said, has lived a rather rapid life, even for a stage girl She is quite handsome, and by some considered beautiful, but her associations have been anything but the best and Caesar Young, whom she is alleged to have murdered, is a fair sample of the men that she has trotted with since she has been a foot light dazzler." That editor concluded with a thought that also comprised the title of the editorial; "Gay actress too gay." There was no question mark in the phrase.

Another opinion piece was delivered in the form of a humorous editorial in a New York City newspaper. It took the form of a juror in the Grand Jury who arrived home and was then grilled by his children about the case. At one point one of the children commented to the father; "If they have no more proof than what was published in the papers, then they must discharge her at once."

If smearing Nan in print was a regular feature of the news cycle following the case, and it certainly was, then the whereabouts of the Smiths would come and go over many, many months of time, before thee Smiths finally resurfaced, from a very long "disappearance." On June 17 it was reported that the District Attorney's office in New York had received word that the Smiths were in the city of Washington D. C. After leaving New York City it was said they went to New Jersey and after remaining there in hiding the couple went on to Washington, arriving in that community on Thursday June 16. They were reported to be under surveillance and the question of extraditing the Smiths was under consideration.

One day after that report of the location of the Smiths, a different Washington D. C., paper contradicted the above account. A spokesman for the Washington Police Department told the reporter for the second newspaper; "No, the Morgan Smiths are not here, neither have the New York police ever requested us to look out for them." He added; "Personally I do not think they are in Washington, nor do I believe any New York detectives are here shading them. My belief is that the New York police know where they really are, and have given reporters the idea that the couple came to Washington for the purpose of getting them off the track." The idea there being that if the Smiths read such stories [about being in Washington when they were not] the couple could become a little careless in whatever city they were really hiding in. J. Morgan Smith was described herein was an insurance agent.

With respect to the strength of the case one observer remarked; "As it stands, the case of the government is weak and the absence of any direct knowledge by the law officers of the shooting will make it extremely difficult to get a conviction. Every day or so a story is printed of the finding of a witness to the shooting, but little credence is placed in any of them by the authorities."

Assistant District Attorney Rand regarded the Smiths as "important witnesses" and he told the press that he would not put Patterson on trial until he had apprehended those witnesses. Detectives were then said to be looking for them in several cities but authorities in New York admitted they had no idea where the couple might be. That pronouncement seemed to end any faint hope that Nan might have entertained for a speedy trial. Another report that same day stated that Detective Price of the New York Police Department and pawnbroker Stern journeyed to Washington in the hopes of seeing Smith. When they arrived in that city two Washington police department detectives joined them and all four wandered around the town for hours in the fruitless hope of just bumping into Smith on the street. By then Stern, reportedly, had already identified a photograph of Smith as the male half of the couple that supposedly purchased the weapon from him, but Rand was seeking a "more positive" identification, one based upon a live person.

Meanwhile, Nan's prison life was described as "monotonous." The only visitors she then received, besides her lawyers, was her father. John Patterson visited several times a day, brought her fruit and other items otherwise unobtainable. Her negro maid, mentioned in an earlier piece was identified herein as Mrs. Izzy White, a black woman who was also a prisoner in the Tombs awaiting a trial for murder. It was said that White; "acts as her maid, arranging her coiffure every morning." A reporter who was allowed in for an interview with Patterson told his readers that each mail brought "scores" of letters to her. As well, hundreds of people had been to see her in person, but not had got near her. As background to the interview the journalist remarked; "It is well known about the district attorney's office that the government has little or no case against her and is not anxious to go to trial, hoping something will develop in the meantime." He also noted that the pistol and its ownership was considered a crucial piece of evidence and that another theory under some level of consideration was that Young tried to commit suicide and, after a scuffle with Nan, succeeded. "No one advanced any belief that Nan Patterson deliberately killed Caesar Young," asserted the interviewer. By now Nan Patterson's fame had grown to the point where she was immortalized, sort of. One of New York City's dime museums was called the Eden Musee and it had a section called the "World of Wax." That institution was proud to announce a new addition to its wax figures on public display on June 26, just three weeks after the tragedy – Nan Patterson.

Actresses were up in arms over the Patterson case, or so it seemed from an opinion piece that appeared in a Minnesota newspaper. The article appeared on the dramatic and amusement page and declared that actresses who "have some regard for their good name" were upset with regard to the treatment of that case in New York. "This notorious woman, whose single claim to histrionic notice was that she appeared briefly" as a member of a *Floradora* company that toured the west two or three seasons ago and "is continually referrer to in the press as an actress," fumed the journalist. "This may cast the glamour of the footlights about the central figure of this tragedy, but it is eminently unfair to the members of the profession who are really actresses."

The never-ending saga of the Smiths continued on July 7 when it was said to be understood that Smith had returned to Washington and Assistant District Attorney Rand had sent one of his men to the nation's capital to apprehend him. Meanwhile, one of Smith's lawyers was cited as having agreed to produce Smith "at the proper time."

Mrs. Smith (Nan's sister Julia) was said to be in Washington at the Patterson family home early in July, according to neighbors. That report was actually true. On July 6 Mrs. Smith called on Frederick E. Rittman, Auditor for the United States War Department in reference to reinstatement in her old position of clerk in his office. Julia Patterson (as she was) "had a good record in the Government service, and is highly spoken of by Mr. Rittman," said a journalist. In the spring of 1903 she had taken two months' vacation from that job to travel and before the two months were up she had met and married Smith. She then resigned from her post. When Julia went to see Rittman on July 6 the latter pointed out to her the rules governing her situation. A year had not passed since her resignation took effect and according to civil service rules she was entitled to have her name placed on the eligible list, subject to appointment to any vacancy. However, there was then no vacancy in her old department. Therefore Julia was sent to the Civil Service Commission to place her application on file. Julia Smith resigned her clerkship position (it paid $1,700 annually) in the Auditor's office on August 15 1903 in order to marry J. Morgan Smith. Mr. Smith was said to then be in poor health and Julia needed the money to help support him. A brief report that appeared in the newspaper on July 19 stated only that Julia was unsuccessful in gaining reinstatement with the United States government and had left the city of Washington.

Late in July Nan Patterson told her story and it appeared first in the *New York American*. Said Nan; "The truth is that the bullet that killed Mr. Young was meant for me. But the motion of the cab and a hand unsteadied by a night's carouse saved my life." When a reporter asked her if that was the story she would tell the jury she said it was; "Mr Young shot himself while trying to shoot me. He had intended to kill me first and, no doubt, he meant to commit suicide afterward; but he had been drinking heavily and his hand was unsteady. His aim was uncertain and he shot himself instead of me." She further explained that on Saturday morning June 4 Nan and her sister were awakened by the telephone ringing. Julia answered and she said Nan was asleep and she did not want to wake her. She hung up the phone but it rang again after a few minutes. (Earlier Nan had told the reporter that Young "had threatened his own life and mine many times.") Julia woke Nan up and told her she would have to get up; "He is determined to see you. He wants you to meet him at the [Columbus] Circle and drive to the pier with him." He had been drinking all night. Young asked her if she would sail on the following Tuesday or Wednesday and join him in Europe. She said no as she would be lonely during all the time he was with his wife. Nan portrayed Caesar as in despair and disconsolate about their pending separation, and so on. Nan said they stopped the cab three times during the journey, twice so Caesar could get a drink at a bar and once so he could buy a hat. According to her, Young's partner John Millin had been picked out of the "gutter" by Young and was always jealous of her and that she would get more money from Young than he would. She declared she had never written threatening letters and hardly wrote to him at all, worried her letters might fall into the hands of the wife. Patterson said she joined the B company of *Floradora* in the fall of 1901 and finished the season as a member of the sextet. Then company manager Mr. Fisher sent her to Chicago to join the sextet of another company, for six weeks in the summer of 1903. And after that she was briefly with the Harrington Reynolds' stock company at Los Angeles.

Efforts to get Patterson released from detention on habeas corpus proceedings or out on bail continued in this period, but always to no avail. Lawyers Henry Unger and Abraham Levy argued for an early date for the trial, however, the prosecution insisted it would wait until the Smiths returned to New York City before a trial date was set. A motion for Nan to be released on her own recognizance was, of course, denied by the court.

Then, somewhat surprisingly, a writ of habeas corpus for Patterson was granted on August 31, returnable on the following day. That writ ordered the warden of the Tombs to produce his prisoner in the Supreme Court at which time her counsel would ask for her discharge on the ground that there was no evidence she committed the crime. If that was denied an application would be made that the detainee be entitled to bail.

On the following day New York State Supreme Court Justice Amend decided to grant bail – in the amount of $20,000. However, he added that if District Attorney Jerome would consent to accept bail in a lesser amount, he would lower the sum to $15,000 or even to $10,000. Lawyers for Nan complained that the high amount of bail would be impossible to raise. Levy explained that Jerome agreed with the request for bail although the two sides differed on the amount of the bail. Levy suggested $10,000 while Assistant District Attorney Sandford asked for $20,000.

The possibility that Patterson might be freed shortly, at least until her trial, spurred on at least one member of the entertainment industry to make a pitch for her services. In the evening, after the announcement allowing a bail amount there came a statement from F. Ray Comstock in New Haven Connecticut, manager of the stage production *The Runaways*, which was then opening in that city at the Hyperion Theatre. Comstock declared that he had just received word from counsel for Nan, accepting his offer to put her into *The Runaways*. Acceptance was conditional, according to Comstock, on a "slight increase" in the salary that had been already offered. That increase, Comstock declared, would be made by him. He hoped that she would be soon released from detention and thus join his show within a few days, in time for the production's opening in New York City at Proctor's Theatre. However, later that day Abraham Levy stated everything about the job offer with respect to *The Runaways* was a lie. "Miss Patterson when released," he said, "will seek some quiet spot where she can recuperate and regain the strength she has lost in her long imprisonment."

A dispatch from New York City on September 6 stated that John H. Vandervoort, a lawyer, appeared at the District Attorney's office that day with deeds and mortgages representing $3 million in value and offered to give bail to Nail. He had an interview with the woman in the Tombs and told her he would spend his fortune to obtain her acquittal. Assistant District Attorney Miner looked over the securities and refused to accept them.

A slightly different version of the story appeared in a different newspaper and showed that all the "silly season" characters that crawled out into the light with regard to this case were not all "eye-witnesses." When Nan opened her mail a day earlier she found a letter from John Vandervoort who explained that he had taken a deep interest in her case and if somebody would come up to see him, at 250 West 144th Street, he would be happy to bail her out. Nan's father made the trip to see him. Then Mr. Patterson took him to the bail bureau at the District Attorney's office. Vandervoort was shabbily dressed and his papers were only about court decisions affecting certain properties in the area in which he resided. He didn't own any of those properties. He had, in the past, given over pots of his "millions" to charities such as the Salvation Army. In short, Vandervoort was poor and delusional.

More parts of Nan's "own story" was reprinted in various newspapers, having first appeared in the *New York American*. That story was said to have come "through an intimate friend, Miss Hope Booth" and through that source Nan had made "a most remarkable statement for the [William Randolph] Hearst newspapers." Reportedly Nan said that Young deceived her as to his marriage and when she learned how his wife really loved him, she tried to induce him to remain faithful. She denied she wanted him to stay in America and claimed his proposed voyage to Europe was a relief to her. She offered this advice to young girls; "Keep away from married men!" Added Nan; "When a girl falls in love she doesn't take time to consider whether the man is married until it is too late." With regard to her routine in prison Patterson declared; "We are ordered out of our cells at 6:30 o'clock and supper at 4. Right after supper I'm locked in my cell and there I remain until 6:30 the next morning. I try to be as nice as I can to my companions here when I am with them. I don't like to be holding aloof. Still there are some elements here that can't be altogether congenial to me – and oh, my God, it's awful." As a further thought, she continued; "But for a married man I would not have been here. He did not love his wife, but he did love me. I did not know he had a wife at first, but when I learned of it I tried to have him go back to her. When he told me he was going to Europe I was glad, for she was going with him."

On September 12 1904 Nan Patterson turned 22 years of age and a celebration of sorts was held in and around her cell. Her father and brother arrived at the Tombs carrying birthday presents for her. However, father John Patterson said that he had not been able to raise bail. It was also reported that District Attorney Jerome was then willing to have the bail amount reduced to $10,000.

Later in September, in was reported on the 27th, that through the efforts of boxer Young Corbett Patterson would be released as early as that afternoon on $10,000 bail. In anticipation of the release a "large crowd" gathered around the Tombs that day, in hopes of seeing Nan. That announcement was made by Maurice Meyer of the law firm of which Daniel O'Reilly (one of the woman's lawyers) was a member. It was declared that Corbett had agreed to furnish money "on the urgent representations of the girl's friends," and John Patterson believed it was all arranged.

Yet on the very same day, in a different Washington D. C. newspaper, appeared an account claiming the opposite was true. Herein it was remarked that through the efforts of John Patterson wealthy friends in Washington became convinced Nan was not guilty and agreed to assist in finding bail, stipulating that their names should not be mentioned. The bail amount, herein $20,000, was to be furnished by a "well-known surety company" of Washington. John Patterson's friends suggested that some surety company would furnish the bond if it was insured against the danger of losing its money to a forfeit. Accordingly, an indemnity was given to insure the New York company. No mention was made of Corbett Young.

One day later it was noted that the effort made by Corbett and other friends of Nan met with failure. One of the members of O'Reilly's firm said that assurances had been given that Jerome would accept $10,000 as sufficient bail. Efforts were then made to get the money from a large New York City trust company. One day after that it was remarked that a bond by a surety company for $20,000 was refused, on September 28, by the District Attorney's office. The ground for refusal of the bond was said to be "because the law exacts an element of personal responsibility. The district attorney advised the surety company indemnity personal bondsmen." With logic like that, however, no bail would ever be sufficient and/or ever accepted. With that move the state clearly indicated that Nan Patterson would never be released on bail, not matter what the amount and no matter who furnished it.

Problems with bail for the detainee prompted a Washington D. C., newspaper to editorialize on the subject. That editor observed that she had not gotten the speedy trial as guaranteed by the Constitution. He went on to note that her experiences should be a lesson to thousands of her type who haunted the metropolis; "A handsome, gay, and careless girl, with no more intellectual prowess than impels the flitting butterfly, she sought any company that seemed congenial, no idea of consequences or morals entering her head." As far as the editor was concerned the fact that Young was under the influence of alcohol at the time meant he could have shot himself and, in any event, the truth would probably never be determined. Concluded the editor; "Nan Patterson suffers for having violated the tenets of decency. As said before, her experience should be a lesson to others. But it won't be." This editorial was one of the first ones to pontificate that the woman had to suffer and be punished because she violated a moral code and a decency that was promulgated by the ruling class, and of which violations by that ruling class were ignored and unpunished, while those of the underclass were often held up for public scorn and then punished. While the editorial was the first of that kind it would not be the last. Ann Elizabeth Patterson had to be punished because she was a young female who was "loose," who engaged in adultery, who, albeit briefly, engaged in a profession (acting) that was viewed by the ruling class as only slightly above that of prostitute, and interacted freely with the opposite sex without going through the rituals of a formal introduction, using a chaperon, and so forth. She had to be and was punished for all those "indecencies." Whether or not she murdered Frank Thomas Young was not especially relevant.

On October 3 1904 all branches of the General Sessions Courts reopened in New York after the summer vacation, reviving the idea that Nan might soon come to trial. On that date there were 505 persons under indictment, of whom 334 were out on bail. There were 18 homicide cases to be tried. The oldest untried indictment was that of Ann Elizabeth Patterson.

John Patterson told his daughter around that time that he was doing all he could to post bail but he could not find anybody to post such a high bond. It was also noted that the prosecution had not moved away from its position that no trial would be held until the Smiths were found. Lawyers for Nan reiterated the fact that they did not know the whereabouts of the couple.

The delay in bringing the woman to tried generated an editorial in a Washington D. C., paper, in the middle of October. Observing that Jerome has promised Nan that she would be tired during the November term of the court the editor went on to mention that lack of a speedy trial to that point and the problem of the Smiths. As far as this newsman was concerned the blame for the disappearance of the couple "was solely the fault of the State, and that to cause the penalty to fall upon the prisoner was a wrong so palpable that there can be no harm in mentioning it." Noting that sometimes the presumption of innocence was a fiction but; "In the case of Miss Patterson the presumption had a substantial basis. There was doubt of her guilt in the beginning and this has increased as the season passed, and the prosecution showed throughout fear of the trial eagerly sought by the prisoner." Concluded the editor; "The tardiness of Miss Patterson's trial becomes a public grievance, because there is no reason to suppose that it is exceptional."

And then, at the end of October, as if to keep the case of Patterson alive and full of new headlines came yet another in a seemingly endless line of "eye-witnesses." This time it was not one but two, as the silly season got even sillier, if that were possible. News was reported on October 31 that two men who, enthused a so-called journalist, "are among the first citizens in the communities in which they live and are well known in business" claimed they saw Caesar Young kill himself. At the time of the shooting one of those two witnesses swore the other to secrecy and took a vow himself that he would not tell what he saw. Why, the curious reader might have asked? Because, explained the writer of that piece; "there was no good reason why they should be in the city and that it was against their business interests that their presence here should be known." This new "revelation" caused the reporter to confidently predict that Nan would be released from custody no later than the following afternoon.

On the following day one of those two men was identified. Milton W. Hazelton was described as a prominent businessman of Oneonta, Oswego County, New York, and was one of the two. He went to District Attorney Jerome's office and declared in an affidavit that he saw Young fire the fatal shot. He said the other man was with him at the time but he did not know his identify of the second man as he was a chance acquaintance. Hazelton explained he was attracted by the Masonic emblem on the other man's watch chain, leading the pair to engage in a conversation. Hazelton, 78 years old, claimed he came forward when he did because he had become conscience stricken, although at the time of the shooting the pair agreed they did not wish to be detained as witnesses and agreed to say nothing. When taken to West Broadway by police Hazelton could not identify the area where shooting took place.

A little more detail abut Hazelton was revealed a day later. Hazelton said that he came back to New York City in September and tried to see Nan in the Tombs. Admittance was refused him because he did not have a pass; he was advised to go the District Attorney's office to procure a pass. He said he went there but was told to see the woman's attorneys. Hazelton did so and was told that what he had seen made him a valuable witness. Then he went home to Oneonta feeling that he had not received proper consideration. Subsequently he wrote a letter, addressing it "To Nan Patterson's Father, New York." And; "He heard nothing from this letter, but says that he understands it reached its destination."

An editorial published on November 2 was another one to stress the need for Nan to be punished, and not only for the death of Young; it also addressed the subject of the "eye-witnesses" that kept surfacing. Said the editor; "Vainly she has sought to be placed on trial. There never has been general belief in her guilty although her indiscretions throughout her career has been glaring. She is accused of killing Caesar Young, a man whose affections she had won away from his wife. Her case was not one to excite maudlin sympathy, for the girl deserved punishment." With respect to the latest witness, the editor offered the opinion that; "If the story can be substantiated, of course there is nothing to be done in relation to the prisoner except to give her freedom." He added that the difficulty came in believing that a man could hardly be imagined so mean as to be in possession of such knowledge and keep it suppressed; "even friends of the prisoner will concede that this eleventh hour yarn does not impress...If the witness speaks the truth, he is making a confession of heartlessness most abnormal. His conscience is of a type so markedly somnolent that wonder exists that ever it had an awakening."

Notwithstanding Hazelton's statement that he saw Young commit suicide Nan was to still be put on trial – he had told his story to the District Attorney's office twice. Herein Hazelton said that the reason he withheld testimony for so long was that he was afraid of being locked up in the House of Detention. But ever since the day of the shooting his conscience had bothered him and eventually caused him to come forward and make a clean breast of things.

The New York Press published an interview with Nan on November 2 where it said that Young meant to murder Patterson and then kill himself. And, in a slap at the Hearst newspapers, and others, Nan explained to this interviewer; "Interviews have been printed in newspapers, but they were all lies. I never gave an interview to anyone, and the stuff which I was made to say was ridiculous. In fact, most of the statements made in the newspapers about my life were incorrect. Why, the only time I broke down since my imprisonment was when I read an interview said to have been given by me. The statements in the so-called interview were so far from the truth that I became hysterical when I read them." Nan added that the idea that she followed Young around to various parts of the country was wrong; Caesar was after her all the time.

And still another "witness" popped up, as of November 3. John Latour, on that date, was incarcerated in the Tombs. He was awaiting sentence for stealing a wagon. He was then claiming to be the mysterious man who supposedly jumped onto the step of the hansom cab back on June 4. He then went home, on June 4, and told his wife about the incident; she advised him not to say anything about it so he kept quiet. A reason Latour had not come forward earlier was that he said he feared his employer would learn that he had once been in prison and fire him. The wagon incident was at least the second offense for Latour.

Reportedly, Daniel O'Reilly, lawyer for Nan, went to the Tombs and had a long talk with her. He warned her to make no more statements, under any circumstances. A problem with that was the fact that, as Nan had stated earlier, the press regularly made up interviews that had never taken place, and to attribute quotes to Patterson, in other contexts, that had never happened. Those quotes made up part of the interviews Nan "gave" to the press; the interviews that had never taken place at all.

Finally, a court date was set for the trial. On the morning of November 7 Judge Vernon M. Davis of the criminal branch of the New York State Supreme Court, on application from Assistant District Attorney Rand, fixed November 15 as the date for the start of the trial. Nan was in court for only about a minute. A reporter noted; "Since her last appearance in public she has gained between twenty and twenty-five pounds in weight. She looked happy and was seemingly confident of the final outcome."

Beautiful Young Woman Whose Part In the Mystery Shrouding the
Death of Caesar Young In a Cab Is Still Unexplained

Portrait of Patterson, published on June 10 1904. Note that she was again misnamed as Mrs. Nan Patterson

CHAPTER 4. TRIAL #1.

Prosecution of Ann Elizabeth Patterson was to be led by Assistant District Attorney William Rand with assistance from Assistant Deputy Francis Garvan. For Nan, Abraham Levy would be the senior counsel assistance by Daniel O'Reilly and Philip Waldheimer. The trial was expected to last about one week. The Smiths had still not been located.

In the lead up to the trial another smear item appeared against the woman. A Washington D. C., newspaper declared that; "It was learned that Nan Patterson has been attended by a fashionable dressmaker for two weeks and it is expected that her costumes will cause something of a sensation when she appears in court. The visits of the dressmaker have been kept very quiet. The prisoner obtained permission to have the dressmaker go to her cell and asked that her visits be kept secret. This wish has been respected, and no one will say very much concerning the new dresses, except an attendant, who admitted they were 'stunning.' She has also purchased a collection of hats." As an aside the article asserted that Mrs. Smith was in New York City and Julia had made a couple of recent visits to the Tombs to see her sister. All of the above was a lie.

A New York City newspaper took up the dresses idea and was more accurate. That account had it that Nan told a reporter for the *Evening World* she she had gotten so fat she could not get any of her dresses on, for the trial. "So I had to have a new one and my dressmaker was here this morning and will be here again this afternoon to fit it. It is just a plain black gown..." Nan denied that Mrs. Smith had visited. A woman did come to the Tombs, said she was Mrs. Smith, sister of Nan, and wanted to see her. She was not allowed to visit but sent in a note. Patterson said the visitor was unknown to her, and was definitely not her sister Julia. Patterson did need a new dress for the trial because she had gained some weight. The dressmaker came once, with the dress. She met Nan in the common area, not in her cell. Nan's cell, and all the others inhabited by women in the Tombs, was literally too small for such activity. All of those cells were inhabited by one female. The single dress she acquired was a simple black one.

After a delay of one day the trial got officially underway on Wednesday November 16, 1904. The courtroom was jammed full of the curious and an extra squad of police officers was on hand to reinforce the court officers in their efforts to control the crowd. Nan's father John sat with her at the defence table, as he would for every day of the trials. Lawyers defending Patterson were Abraham Levy, Daniel O'Reilly, Henry Unger and Philip Waldheimer. The defendant was described as "pale and nervous," even though the prevailing opinion, according to one journalist; "is that the girl will be acquitted."

On the day before the trail began, Rand reportedly sent people from his office out to go around town and collect photographs of J. Morgan Smith. The Smiths still had not been found and it was thought Rand would use photographs of Smith, in lieu of the real person, to show on the stand to pawnbroker Stern, in order to get an identification of Smith as the gun buyer. However, the District Attorney's office had already shown at least one photograph of Smith to Stern, with a failure to identify.

Another smear and blatant lie was published on November 16 and purported to be a description of Nan as she entered the courtroom on the first day of the trial; "Gowned as if she were

out for a morning walk along 5th avenue, New York, Miss Patterson stepped jauntily into the court room at 10 o'clock. In a new and handsome dress of black voile, black hat and with double flowing veil, she was a picture of healthful womanhood. No ghastly prison pallor was on her face...For aught her manner disclosed she was in court as spectator instead of prisoner at the bar."

In a separate article in the same newspaper as above an article purported to tell of Patterson's morning at the Tombs. Yet it too, was all false. A direct quote attributed to Nan that morning declared; "I am more pleased than I can express that my trial is underway. I am so confident of the outcome,,," and it continued on it that manner. It amounted to two large paragraphs, mostly quotes. However, no journalists were in her cell or the common area that morning. Sometime after 9:00 AM she would have been taken from her cell and escorted across the street for the 10:00 AM court session. Talking to a reporter did not take place. The criminal courts building and the Tombs were directly across the street from each other and access for prisoners and police escorts back and forth was along a closed overpass, known by its nickname, the "Bridge of Sighs." No reporters were allowed through that passageway. A prisoner was not escorted back and forth at street level unless, of course, the authorities wanted to display and shame their detainee.

Another description of the prisoner when the trial began went as follows; "The face is not attractive either in repose or when, as it frequently was today, contracted by laughter or smiles. Her eyes are small and of hazy sluggish blue, devoid of luster. Altogether she was an ordinary appearing young woman who looked as if she might be employed in a Sixth avenue shop." And, it continued; "When called to the bar she walked awkwardly through the court room aisle with a gait somewhat theatrical in intent, but which developed into a strut before she slid down into her chair." A large crowd clamored to get in to watch the proceedings because, wrote a reporter; "there is to be brought out the inside doings of a certain theatrical set and of racetrack life." On the first day of the trial 25 talesmen were examined and four of them were selected to be on the juror.

Assistant District Attorney Rand admitted, as the trial got underway, that he had no direct evidence of the shooting; that is, no witnesses to the event and that he had to depend on circumstantial evidence. With respect to the four jurors selected by the end of the first day all were married men and all stated that relations between Caesar and Nan not "sanctioned by law" would not prejudice them against her. As well, all were asked for their views on capital punishment applied to women; none were opposed to it. In that "special veniremen" of 100 potential jurors appeared, noted a report, "the names of men well known in business and society," with many of those names actually listed in the story. As for Nan's appearance; "She wore a black gown and a black hat. When she saw the crowd, the Judge and the assemblage of lawyers and reporters her step faltered for a moment, but she recovered herself and walked down the room firmly, her head bowed and her eyes downcast."

Another false line of attack against the defendant took the form of making the bizarre claim that it was Patterson herself who was calling the shots with regard to the selection of the jury members. The story went that she either played a large role in that selection or that she controlled it entirely herself. It was all, of course, nonsense. She was a young woman who had just turned 22 and this was her first court experience. She had four lawyers, all men and all much older and, obviously, experienced. The idea that Nan selected the jury – and that point was made for all the trials – was not just a lie, it was a ludicrous lie. A headline from a November 17 article on the trial asserted; "Nan Patterson selects jurors." The text of that article took a softer line by declaring; "Nan Patterson herself had aided in their selection, objecting to this or that man, finally acquiescing in the judgment of her lawyers." Reportedly, the question that gave potential jury members the most trouble was the following; "If it should appear that the defendant had led an improper or meretricious [attracting attention in a vulgar manner] life with the deceased for a period of years, knowing that he had a wife living, would that fact serve to prejudice your mind against her in arriving at your verdict?" Giving the defendant even more "control" could be found in another article wherein it stated; "Whenever Miss Patterson disapproves of a talesman who is satisfactory to both counsel [each side], her lawyers promptly reject the man."

One talesman questioned was Archibald C. C. Anderson, a 58-year-old retired merchant. When Rand asked if he had talked to anyone about the case he said to Judge Vernon Davis that he knew of a person who had witnessed the tragedy but who shrank from coming forward as a witness. He was promptly excused from the jury panel, and yet another "eye-witness" was born. After a brief conversation with Anderson, lawyer O'Reilly said he had valuable information for the defense and promised to produce the eye witness. According to the story the son of Anderson told his father there was a young woman employed where he, the son, worked whose brother had witnessed the shooting. Anderson said he had talked to the brother. At that point O'Reilly was said to have the name of the brother but would not reveal it. In attendance at the trial was John Millin. Herein it said that Nan was made nervous by his presence "and asked that Millin be compelled to sit back of her." The court then told Millin to move to the rear of the courtroom, or so the account would have its readers believe. It was a lie.

One of the potential jurors who was being questioned was grinning. Nan's lawyer Abraham Levy asked him if he had ever known John Millin. The man said no and grinned. Millin was made to walk up to the bar (from the back where he was already sitting) to stand before the potential juror so that man could identify him and affirm that he had never seen Millin before. And, said a journalist; "As Millin passed Nan Patterson those in court expected something to happen, but Millin hardly looked at her or she at him." That was all there was to the Millin incident.

Another news item contained a description of Nan in the courtroom on the second day; "There was nothing in her appearance to show she had spent a troubled night, and her rich black dress bore evidence that she had made a careful toilette before appearing before the court. As she stepped into the room she glanced at her jurors who were selected yesterday to try her, and her look showed confidence and satisfaction" Then the piece moved into pure fabrication. It described her father John arriving that morning before court began and the two of them having breakfast together in her cell and reading the newspaper coverage of the trial. John visited his daughter daily but would not have been allowed in before a court session. Nan's single occupancy cell was about four feet by ten feet and contained no furniture except a bed and a bucket for the cold water pipe.

A report published the results of its survey as to the guilt of Patterson. "Several members of the legal profession, when questioned, unofficially, today, regarding the status of the case, expressed the opinion privately that Miss Patterson was innocent and would be acquitted. They said they believed she had simply been held in deference to public sentiment. There was no doubt in their minds that Young committee suicide in a fit of despondency."

The twelfth and last man was selected to the jury on November 18, after the defence had used up all but two of their peremptory challenges. A total of 89 talesmen had been examined. In describing Nan this account said; "She fairly swept into the court-room...Her step had a fresh spring in it that was almost a dance...Inspired with courage by the rapid accumulation of evidence in her favor she slept soundly throughout the night and ate a hearty breakfast." The author of that piece had no way of knowing, of course, how she slept the night before in her cell. This account added that in dismissing one prospect "Miss Patterson told Mr O'Reilly that she would prefer to have hustlers on the jury." In this case, also, no reporter could have overheard such a conversation between Nan and O'Reilly at the defense table. A different account maintained the fiction that; "She scrutinized each talesman, and no juror was accepted by her counsel against her advise." No lawyer would ever allow such control over jury selection by an inexperienced 22-year-old who, in any case, had not been socialized to talk back to, and overturn the decisions of, older men.

With the jury of 12 men selected and sworn in it was speculated that the panel may not have been entirely satisfactory to

Rand. The journalist speculated that; "Ever since the selection of a jury was begun sleuths from the district attorney's office have been quietly making investigations to ascertain if there was any reason other than could be learned in court why jurors were not qualified to serve." Also reported was that Nan had received 22 letters from the first mail in her cell in the Tombs that day. Four of them were said to be from men who wanted to marry Patterson. Her father John stated that; "She has had hundreds of letters from men who are anxious to marry her."

Monday, November 21, 1904 was the first day of the trial with evidence taken. Anticipating the coming trial one article had subheads describing what was to come; "Gay and wicked life of cities will be brought to the fore," and "The turf world, the cafe world and others to be explored." Rand began by outlining the state's case during which he dwelt on the relationship between Young and the defendant and the alleged motives. Nan sat through the proceedings "with tense expression, while every now and then she convulsively clutched her father's hand when the prosecutor cut her to the quick with some stinging reference to her character." Said Rand, to the jury; "Now gentlemen of the jury the manner of living of this young woman must not be held against her. Her chastity and virtue are not on trial here...Of course her dependence on the dead man is of the highest importance and must be considered." He continued; "We will show all the manners of the turf world and its life; the Broadway Cafe and its gay life; the all night cafe and the night rides through the city – all will be shown you." Briefly he told of Caesar's life – admitting that he drank heavily and would frequently at the track drink 30 glasses of beer and every morning he would have three or four drinks of brandy at breakfast. "Young was a man who exercised a singularly great influence on women and he was himself easily susceptible to women." It was noted that the man ran around a lot. In the fall of 1902 Young went west alone and on the train to California he met Nan. At that time she was a married woman with her divorce not yet granted. They left the train at Chicago, intimately connected, and later traveled to California together as man and wife. Rand continued his outline of the couple by remarking that in the spring of 1904 the pair went on a "debauch" in Berkeley California and then went to Los Angeles where races were being run. Mrs. Young followed them to Los Angeles after sending word to John Millin to locate them. He found them recovering from a debauch in a Turkish bath in Los Angeles. Mrs. Young came there and there followed a scene. Mrs. Young insisted the affair must end and the pair had to separate. Millin took Nan to the train station, bought her a ticket to New York City, and gave her $800 in cash. That was in March 1904. Nan left. That was a first attempt at breaking the couple up. However, it did not work and the pair soon started seeing each other again. Then came plans to split them up with the trip to Europe.

An opinion piece that appeared in various newspapers at this time was written by W. B. Bat Masterson, promoter of prize fights, and "all-round sport," formerly of the West-at-large, but then residing in New York City. It was THE Bat Masterson who went on to fame decades later with that character being the basis for the television series *Bat Masterson*, that ran from 1958-1961. His piece was written during jury selection and, wrote Masterson; "The entire proceeding appears to me as nothing short of a farce-comedy, enacted for the benefit of the morbidly curious and for the purpose of giving a few lawyers a chance to gain a little notoriety through the press." Noting that prosecution had no witnesses and Nan was the only person who knew what really happened he went on to add; "I presume the trial of Nan Patterson is a public necessity, if not a public benefit, and had the prosecuting attorney's office declined to prosecute because of the lack or insufficiency of the evidence, it would have been censured severely by press as well as public." Masterson explained that he knew Caesar Young and liked him; "His friends repeatedly tried to induce him to break off the alliance with the show girl, but he stubbornly refused to do so. He practiced all manner of deception of his lawful wife in order to be with the Patterson woman." And, he asserted; "I can see no good reason for wasting sympathy on Caesar Young. He was a good fellow, and it is too bad he met such an untimely death; but there seems to be no one to blame but himself. Nan Patterson will undoubtedly be acquitted – just as she should be...” He concluded by noting; “Nan Patterson was never anything but a show girl – which, I understand, is one point higher in the show business than the chorus girl.”

Some reality about Patterson's wardrobe came from the pen of journalist Katherine Leckie, who wrote; “A great deal has been said lately about the magnificence of the wardrobe of Nan Patterson and the numerous dresses that have been prepared for her appearance in court. It has even been hinted that she was to dress the part elaborately and that a change of costume was to be frequently made.” Leckie added; “She has each day come in the same somber black gown, and the truth is it is the only winter frock she has, and it was made at the suggestion of her attorney, Mr. O'Reilly.”

Also in his opening remarks Rand told the jury that it should not be swayed by the fact that Nan was a woman – the law was made for men and women alike. Rand declared that Patterson fired the fatal shot and that it was deliberate and premeditated. Then Rand confidently predicted he would prove that. Regarding Young's character Rand said; “He possess traits that a man ought not to be proud of, but he had other traits that will recommend him to you.” When Rand laid out before the jury the story of the pistol used in the shooting and J. Morgan Smith, he stated that on June 3 Smith, accompanied by a woman, purchased a revolver at Hyman Stern's pawnshop; “After the purchase of the revolver he was seen quarreling with Nan Patterson near the Sixth avenue pawnshop. He was heard to say to her ‘you must do it,’ and she replied ‘I will not.’ Then Smith slapped his sister-in-law's face and pushed her into the cab and sent her home.”

When Policeman Quinn (one of the first on the scene) took the stand he testified that while conducting Nan to the coroner's office a few hours after the shooting she had begged him to kill her with his club. She explained she could not live without Young; she had nothing else to live for.

When hansom cabdriver Frederick E. Michaels testified he re-iterated that he heard the shot but nothing more. That is, he heard no conversation or other noises from his cab. Apparently he was not asked about people coming out of the woodwork in droves, being eye-witnesses to the tragedy and even jumping onto the step of his cab. Either he was not asked about any of those things or he was asked but it was not reported in any of the press accounts of his testimony. In any case he had told officials earlier that nobody was close enough to his vehicle at the time of the shooting to have seen anything. Margaret Young was notable by her absence from the court proceedings into the death of her husband. Reportedly, she had remained in seclusion since the day of the death, except when she once ap-peared before the Grand Jury. While she was never seen in the courtroom it was said she followed the proceedings from an ad-joining room.

On one of the trial days the prosecution used a human skel-eton as part of its case, supposedly to show the course of the bullet and path the bullet had taken and to show, if one were to believe the prosecution, that the trajectory of the bullet showed it to be impossible for Caesar Young to have committee suicide. Not surprisingly, the appearance of a skeleton in court caused a sensation. One witness who took the stand was able to speak to the subject of the never-ending stream of eye-wit-nesses. William Stemm Jr., was close enough to the event that he directed cabdriver Michaels to the nearest hospital. Stemm was standing on West Broadway and heard a shot just after the hansom cab passed him. He was standing on the other side of the street. While he saw nothing in the cab he also was able to testify that there was nobody else on the street nearby. At the time of the shot Stemm estimated he was about 12 feet away from the vehicle. Meanwhile, the District Attorney's office an-nounced it would "renew" the search for the Smiths.

Reporting on the crowds at the courthouse one account noted

that those crowds clamored for admission to the courtroom and that; "Fully 500 omen tried to gain entrance yesterday, and though mot of them were turned way, a sufficient number got seats to make the courtroom look more like a hall where a high-class musical performance was going on than like a courtroom." Continued the account; "The women also were loud in their chattering and laughter, and Justice Davis had to wan them from the bench that if the noise continued the seats would be cleared."

Expert testimony of physicians was offered by the state to show that Young could not have killed himself. Also, two cab drivers testified to having seen Young abuse Patterson early in the morning hours of June 4 and still another witness, a newsboy, swore that he saw J. Morgan Smith strike Nan in the face on the night of June 3, after Smith had said to her; "You will have to do it," ad she answered; "I won't." Even several days into the trial it still attracted "unusually large crowds" and special details of policemen were required to keep out those who had no business in the courtroom and to maintain order in the building. Any evidence about powder marks on either Young or Nan was inconclusive and/or not available, or the tests were yet to be performed, even though a few pieces of dried skin from Caesar's body were introduced as evidence. One reason for the lack of full forensic testing was that officials doing such examinations, and the autopsy, believed initially that the case was a suicide and not a murder. Those black spots on the skin of Young had been examined but the technician could not determine the cause. Stern and the question of gun ownership fizzled out in court. Stern himself was reported to be ill at home and did not appear in court. Instead a clerk from Stern's pawnshop identified the pistol. The two cab drivers who claimed to have seen the pair in the early morning hours of June 4 (after the Friday evening June 3 meeting between Young and Patterson was breaking up) claimed to have seen Caesar "abuse" Nan and then to have observed Patterson crying in the cab ride. One of those drivers was John Crowley. The other driver was Albert Schneider, who corroborated Crowley's version of events. After the aforementioned scene between the couple Nan got into Crowley's cab and headed for home while Young and his brother-in-law used Schneider's cab. Both men were reported to have been under the influence of alcohol. More bizarre and completely unbelievable was the event supposedly seen by newsboy Joseph Hewitt. On Friday evening at about 9:00 PM, explained Hewitt Smith and Patterson came out of a cafe quarreling and as they got into a cab and J. Morgan Smith struck Nan in the face. The slap in the face came after Smith forcefully told Nan she had to do it and the woman replying that she would not.

Some days into the trial a description of the defendant remarked that; "The little white-faced prisoner is obviously devoid of courage or brutality. She is of the tearful, morbid, selfish type rather than the passionate type. It is hard to imagine such a creature possessed of a grand or heroic emotion. That opinion was based on this journalist's reading of the trial testimony; "Young beat her in the face and cursed her on the night before the tragedy...A few hours before her lover cursed her and beat her she was also sworn at and beaten by her tall brother-in-law, J. Morgan Smith..." Thus, concluded the newsman; "All through these scenes pending the death of her lover, Nan was crying and protesting. But to kill him meant the end of the income, which, it is said, she valued more than anything else."

In another account of the crowd it was stated; "Many women again tried to get into the criminal branch of the supreme court, where the trial is being held, yesterday. On Tuesday the women were dressed in good taste and were apparently of good breeding. Yesterday's delegations wore local clothes, were bedecked with diamonds and chatted incessantly. So loud was the noise that Justice Davis ordered one..." person ejected. No other account mentioned anything at all about the crowd, other than the occasional passing reference to the idea that more people wanted in than the number of seats that were available could accommodate. Certainly no account ever appeared anywhere else about a constantly raucous and unruly crowd of spectators.

Thus the above story was another fabrication and perhaps was published only to display the not so subtle misogyny of the newspaper.

Contrast that description of the courtroom with that published on the same day by a different newspaper. "A large, square, high-ceilinged, well-lighted room, with a soft-spoken, alert young judge in black robes, and the lawyers for and against the prisoner vying with each other in politeness. No harsh words, no wrangling, no levity. The first man in the audience who laughed out at the clumsy utterance of a witness was thrust from the place by order of the judge."

In commenting on the case one newsman declared, on November 24, that; "certainly the case against Nan Patterson begins to look very grave. If Rand continues to the end of the chain he has been weaving the natural end will be conviction," He remarked on the obvious contradiction in the story of Young slapping Patterson, and he wondered why the prosecutor would have used that item because; "This picture hardly jibed with the portrait of Caesar Young drawn for the jury by the prosecutor – the open-handed chivalrous, kind-hearted bookmaker with the high sense of honor he presented as a contrast to the cold-blooded, predatory woman who had fastened herself upon him."

In the Tombs jail where Nan was being held there were then confined to the women's section 43 white women and 13 black women. Two of that group, not counting Nan, were also charged with murder, one white woman and one black female. Patterson continued to be popular, at least in some quarters. According to one report, since the trial began, only eight days earlier, Nan had received four offers of marriage through the mail, two of which came from farmers. Dramatically, a report surfaced on November 25 that J. Morgan Smith was arrested shortly before noon that day in West Nyack New York State by the police. Smith was said to be then locked up in a police cell and that he had been found boarding under a fictitious name with a local family. However, one day later it was report that the Smiths had not been located, let alone arrested.

Then, suddenly, on Saturday November 26 the trial of Patterson was adjourned until Monday November 28 because of the sudden illness of a juror named Edward Dressler – he was seriously ill and it was not expected that he would be able to return, and that meant a mistrial was likely to be declared. And, on Monday November 28 the jury in the case was discharged and a mistrial declared. At the same time District Attorney Jerome served notice that a new jury would be selected and a retrial begun at the term of the court that opened in one week, on Monday December 5.

In the wake of the mistrial one report stated that when the first juror had been selected for the trial, a detective from the District Attorney's office was ordered to keep him in sight at all times "to make sure that he was in no way tampered with." Thus, as each juror was selected he received the same treatment until "twelve men followed the jurors night and day." All of which, of course, was nonsense. Especially in light of a different article published on the same day in the same newspaper. That second article contradicted the first article because it said District Attorney Jerome never had any hope of being able to show that Nan killed Young and thus, shortly before the trial started, he tried to postpone it, admit Nan to a nominal bail and then ignore the case, shelving it permanently. But it was Patterson and her lawyers who insisted on a trial – so she would not be under a stigma from a charge that was never dealt with in court. This article, too, was nonsense, but in a different direction from the first piece. As a last piece of information on trial number one, it was stated that the jury had been polled by the press and that nine stood for acquittal while two were non-committal.

An editorial that summed up trial number one and emphasized Nan's moral failure and that her guilt or innocence did not play much of a role appeared on December 3. The editor declared; "So far as the moral goes it makes little difference whether or not this young woman is guilty of murder. She skated too near the edge. Her relations with this married man spelt danger. These unhallowed relations were such as to lead surely to some humiliating, if not criminal, crisis. The situation meant the ruin of two homes, if not more than that." Thus, trial number one came to an end.

This photo and sketch from October 1904 depicts the prisoner weeping and in despair on her cot in her cell. Or at least the media would often have its readers believe Nan was regularly in such a state; the reality was usually different.

CHAPTER 5. TRIAL #2.

Trial number two started as scheduled, on Monday December 5, 1904, with jury selection. Once again lies were promulgated about Ann Elizabeth Patterson supposedly selecting the jury herself. By December 6 when seven jurors had been selected it was noted that six of them were "gray-haired."

The subhead of one article declared; "Nan Patterson does the choosing herself and selects elderly men." Yet in a second article Patterson was cited as having announced to her lawyers; "I do not want a jury of patriarchs." In a third article Patterson was cited as having said to her lawyer Abraham Levy, as she surveyed the remaining selection of talesmen; "It appears that I will have nothing but grandfathers to select my remaining jurymen from." That article then went on a long-winded supposed verbatim paragraph about her not wanting men over 60, in quotation marks. However, she gave no interviews to those newspapers and her lawyers kept her mute with respect to the press. All the verbatim conversations printed in these accounts were fabrications.

On Thursday December 8 the jury was complete. In total 132 talesmen were examined. The prosecution used 17 of its 30 peremptory challenges while the defense used 27 of its 30 challenges. Rand made his opening statement, which was essentially a rerun of his first opening statement. Apparently, though, it didn't have the same effect on the defendant as it did the first time. Said a journalist; "Hearing herself described as vampire, murderess and a wrecker of homes, the young defendant did not hold down her head and bit her tremulous lips as at her first ordeal."

Public interest in trial number two was just as great as it was for the first trial. "Large crowds gather around the doors of the court room every day, but the ruling of Justice Davis that only those having some connection with the case be permitted to enter has been rigidly enforced up to this time," said a newsman. "Many of the curious ones have not permitted themselves to become discouraged, however, and many remain in the corridors through a greater part of the day, apparently with the expectation that the ban finally will be raised."

During his opening remarks Rand placed less emphasis on the testimony of Hyman Stern, the pawnbroker, than he did at the first trial. Rand was, bizarrely, quoted as saying; "Stern is either keeping back something, or he is a man of the most extraordinary stupidity." Curious would-be courtroom spectators continued to be blocked from attending, "the court remained obdurate in its decision to admit neither women nor men who had no actual business at the proceedings." Over the first few days of the trial the prosecution called all the same witnesses as they did the first time, and the testimony was simply a repeat from the first appearance of these people. One exception occurred when Rand called a surprise witness – Daniel O'Reilly, one of Nan's lawyers. On the stand O'Reilly testified that he knew J Morgan Smith, Mrs. Smith (Nan's sister Julia), and John Patterson (Nan's father) He admitted on the stand that he saw the Smiths on the day of the coroner's inquest – later that day the couple disappeared. And that was all O'Reilly was asked on the stand.

Lies and fabrications by the media, with respect to this case, were never mentioned or criticized by the press in general, or specifically. It was mentioned once in court. On the afternoon of December 12 Justice Vernon M. Davis, stated a journalist, "severely criticized" the attempts by an evening newspaper to obtain interviews with wives of the jurors on the guilt or innocence of the defendant. Said Davis in open court, to the jury; "If such an interview was held or sought it was a gross impropriety and an attempt at subversion of justice in the community. I do not even want to insinuate that those interviews were genuine I do not believe they were." Juror number one stated that a reporter called at his home and endeavored to talk to his wife but was unsuccessful. The foreman of the jury said a reporter attempted to talk to his wife, that "she refused to speak to him and notwithstanding her silence an alleged interview had been published." Other jurors said contact had been attempted by reporters with their wives, but those attempts were unsuccessful.

John Patterson announced on December 13 that as soon as his daughter was freed from her present situation she would devote her life to aiding and helping to uplift chorus girls and other young woman she had met during the past couple of years. He said; "When she is acquitted she will lead an entirely different life from that which has marked her during the last year or two." He envisioned that his daughter would go among those women "who have erred and will show them the error of their ways," adding, "I know she now realizes that the life of a chorus girl is not one that a nice, gentle girl should lead." Concluded John; "No matter what the prosecution brings out I know that at heart my daughter is a thoroughly good and honest girl, and that her heart is true to all that is good."

At that point there was little chance that Patterson would be freed anytime soon. Nevertheless she was still, reportedly, receiving offers to return to show business; offers that ranged all the way from $500 to $1,000 a week and more than one theatrical firm was said to be in the fight for her services. *The Mystery of the Hansom Cab* was one of the stage creations that had been offered to her; it was to reproduce on stage the Caesar Young tragedy. *The Bookmaker's Sweetheart* was the effort of another playwright. That latter piece was a tale of the trial and as a climax Nan went uncomplaining to the electric chair rather than offer testimony to the dishonor of her sweetheart. Other plays, it was said, had also been offered to the prisoner and "agents attempt almost daily to obtain interviews with the prisoner."

On the afternoon of December 13 Rand, perhaps getting more and more desperate, introduced for the first time a bizarre theory that tied the Smiths into the death of Young. As time passed that idea would become more and more important, in the eyes of the prosecution. And that would take place even though there was not the slightest bit of evidence to support the strange idea. That afternoon Rand said he would show Young was killed by Nan as a result of a conspiracy between the actress, her sister Julia (Mrs. Smith) and J. Morgan Smith. He argued the Smiths [still, of course, missing] were accomplices to the crime and that the Smiths disappeared so suddenly that Nan's father John had to take Morgan his clothes, to aid in his escape. Thundered Rand; "I will show that the counsel of this prisoner connived in this escape and that the father of the defendant assisted in it," as he then tried to tie one or another of Nan's lawyers, and her father into the weird plot. As a last point in his theory Rand stated that he believed the Smiths did not expect that murder would be done.

With respect to that theory Rand elaborated by stating the intent was not to kill Young but to do him a wrong. Remarked a journalist; "It has been contended that when Nan got into the cab with Young her scheme was to threaten him and hold him up for more money." However, that theory came crashing down at the opening of the court session of December 14 when Justice Davis ruled out the conspiracy plot outlined by Rand. His ruling prohibited the prosecution from bringing out evidence to back up that theory on the ground that the Smiths were not part of the indictment then being tried; only Nan Patterson stood indicted. At that point that conspiracy theory was dead, at least for trial number two. But it would return for trial number three, when it was pursued to a greater extent.

Pawnbroker Hyman Stern testified on December 13 and it was all a big letdown. He was unable to identify Nan as the woman who accompanied the man who bought the revolver from his store. With respect to the male half of that supposed couple Stern now was not certain if the man had a smooth face or wore a mustache. He was not asked to identify, from the stand, a photograph of J. Morgan Smith. Perhaps because he had failed to do so privately at the police station in earlier times. A photograph of J. Morgan Smith was identified in court by a police officer who testified that he last saw Smith on June 8, the day the couple disappeared.

The widow, Mrs. Margaret Young, was on the stand briefly on December 14 and, inevitably, a comparison between the two females was made in the press. "The spectators could not avoid making comparisons between the two, and it was in the widow's favor. Mrs. Young is tall and handsome, with strong features and a pleasing expression, while her one-time rival in Caesar Young's affections is frail physically, with a small face and a prettiness that is somewhat childish. Her teeth are big and her light blue eyes are very small."

A lengthy character study (read smear) of Nan appeared a day later. Supposedly it was written by one "who has been present throughout the New York murder trial" The piece began by declaring; "The full white throat, the pouty lips, down-drooped at the corners, and the short, heavy-nostrilled nose, suggest a sensual pleasure-loving nature. The cold, gray eye bespeaks a calculating mind. But altogether, it is a face without a trace of the physical characteristics that reveal determination, courage or brutality; a selfish, vain morbid face too weak for heroism, too shallow for passion." And, it continued; One sees in the slight figure that sits all in funeral black beside the careworn, white-haired little old father evidences of the now sub-conscious coquetry, which Nan developed to the full when she lived in the blaze of the footlights, painted and plumed, and moved nightly in a sea of sound and color." Patterson was; "At sixteen a wife, then a luxury-seeking, painted chorus girl, and at twenty-one, a prisoner charged with the murder of the married lover who beat her and cursed her the night before his death...It is difficult to imagine such a creature with courage enough to kill anything but her own soul."

When Margaret Young was on the stand it was revealed she had married Frank Thomas Young on February 7 1891 and her maiden name was Beck. The Beck family made their home at Berkeley California. John Millin testified that first met Nan on

October 10 1902 when she was known as Nan Randolph and that she and his business partner Caesar Young went around together at various race meets in California. On Friday December 16 the prosecution rested its case and the court adjourned until Monday December 19. As of that Friday it was not known whether or not the lawyers for the defense would mount a defense.

A class-based event occurred on Saturday December 17; it had nothing to do with the trial. However, it did involve displaying one of the underclass (Nan) before a member of the ruling class, and a foreign one at that. The United Kingdom's Earl of Suffolk and Berkshire, who was to marry Daisy Leiter, sister of Lady Curzon in Washington D. C., in the following week visited the Washington police headquarters, the criminal courts building and the Tombs jail on December 17. He was accompanied by his sister Lady Katherine Howard and her traveling companion. The Earl said he was interested in the Patterson trial and had read a good deal about it. Assistant District Garvan showed him the skeleton and other evidence from the trial. In the Tombs the Earl saw Nan but did not talk to her. After it was all over the Earl exclaimed; "I've had an awfully good time." He added that he would like to see a session of the trial and officials told him to be on hand Monday. He did show up on Monday and was given a "seat of honor."

It was announced on December 19 that the defense would indeed present witnesses. First witness called was Ida F. Townsend [in chapter 2 she was named as Florence Black], she was the telephone operator at the St. Paul Hotel in New York City when Nan was living their with her sister Julia and the latter's husband (the Smiths). It was Townsend who handled the calls from Young on the morning of June 4. Even Hazelton was called, one of the legion of crazy "eye-witnesses" who popped up after the event to swear he saw the whole thing. He reiterated his delusions but it had no impact. The only witness of any note for the defense, and the witness anticipated by everyone in the court room was Nan Patterson, and she took the stand that afternoon.

In a silent courtroom she described in detail her relations with the dead bookmaker, the trip downtown in the hansom cab that fatal morning in June and of a struggle in which she saw no revolver, of the sound of a pistol shot and the falling of the body of Caesar Young onto her lap. At one point her lawyer Abraham Levy said to Nan; "Tell this jury Nan, did you or did you not shoot Caesar Young." She replied; "I did not and were it in my power to bring him back I would sacrifice my own life to do so." During that cab ride when the pair got back into the vehicle after one of their stops for a drink Caesar asked her if she was coming over [to Europe] to meet him or was she going to quit him. She said it would be better to wait until things quieted down and until he returned from Europe for such decisions. He was upset by those remarks and he grabbed her by the arm and pulled her against him. She struggled to free herself and then "it happened."

Earlier in her testimony, in response to a question from her lawyer Abraham Levy she outlined her earlier relations with Caesar. Ann Elizabeth Patterson was born on September 12 1882 and had turned 22 years old some three months earlier. She went to California in July 1902 and met Young that same month. She was then appearing in the production *Floradora*. She met Young on a train on the way to Los Angeles and soon became intimate. According to her she did not know he was a married man until "some time" after she met him. Supposedly at the suggestion of Young she got a divorce, using a lawyer that Young had told her to use. Nan went east in March 1903 but used to meet Young at different racetracks. When she came east she stayed in New York City for one night with her sister, Julia Smith. The next day she went home to her parents in Washington . But after receiving a telegram from Young she returned to Los Angeles in April 1903, remaining with him for three months. In 1904 she was back in Washington for a visit and left there on May 2 for New York City, where she lived with the Smiths. Young was also in New York City in that month of May but the couple did not see much of each other as he could not easily get away from home and he was trying to settle things with his wife. On June 3 she went to the races with the Smiths and arrived there about 1:00 PM. While at the track the group ran into Young and the couple talked. At that meeting Young told his mistress that Millin and Mrs. Young had "trapped" him and they were going to take him to Europe. He said he didn't want to go but his wife had the money. The Smiths and Nan were back in Manhattan around 6:00 or 7:00 PM at the St. Paul Hotel, where the three lived together. Patterson reiterated that the story told by the newsboy was completely untrue. Caesar called the hotel a few times and in a call her made at 11:00 PM he asked her to met him. She did so and when she met her lover he was with his brother-in-law William Luce. That slap in the face mentioned earlier by the two cab drivers, delivered in the very early morning hours of June 4, was described by Nan as "playful" and a sort of habit. At the end of that meeting, very early on Saturday morning, no arrangement had been made to meet later that day. And later on that Saturday June 4 morning Nan said that Young phoned the St. Paul Hotel three times in his efforts to get her to come out and meet him before his boat sailed.

When journalist Katharine Leckie assessed the testimony of the defendant she declared; "Nan Patterson has made her plea for her wayward life." Mostly this account portrayed Nan as having performed an acting job in the witness box with all of her little moves, and where she looked and who she addressed, and so forth, as being all orchestrated in advance, although Leckie never called her a liar outright. Concluded Leckie; "The voice of Nan Patterson is that of a little child. If the voice portrays the soul within, then this woman, despite her 22 years, is still a child. In it is expressed her immaturity and her under-developed state. Her voice is shrill and piping, and through it she spoke of her relations to the dead bookmaker, told them as though her childish tones had no appreciation of its horror." The media usually referred to her in terms of her emotional, almost hysterical reactions in court and in her cell – but herein she was reduced to almost being a child-like automaton.

In a very different account of Patterson in the dock a journalist stated that Rand had "failed to break down the story of the woman," while she was on the stand. In this account her manner on the stand was described as frank and sincere and that she talked in a low, clear voice, compared to a weak and childish voice that could barely be heard.

Wednesday December 19 was the end of witnesses testifying with the day given over to summations. Abraham Levy took all the morning time to deliver his closing remarks while Rand, for the state, spent the afternoon giving his closing statement. Assistant District Attorney Rand impressed upon the jury that Nan was not being tried for immorality and no woman became bad because of innate depravity. And, wrote a reporter summarizing Rand; "She becomes bad because of the incentives of man and the weakness of her nature." Levy declared that every effort of the prosecution had failed to sustain the charge that Nan pursued and threatened to separate Young from his wife. All the evidence, he emphasized, tended to prove that just the contrary was true."

The case went to the jury on Thursday December 22 but four hours of deliberations produced no results in that afternoon. At 5:00 PM Justice Davis left the courtroom for his home saying he would return to court before 11:00 PM that night if a verdict was reached. Failing that the jury would be locked up for the night. A rumor surfaced at 4:30 PM that the jury stood 10 for acquittal and two for conviction and that the voting had reached a deadlock. Prior to the jury retiring to deliberate a speedy decision had been predicted by many in the media. Also, a huge crowd gathered at the courthouse to hear the anticipated verdict and the New York Police Department was forced to send for 15 policemen in addition to the force of officers already on duty there to control the crowd. When Davis made his charge to the jury one newsman described it by writing; "Justice Davis' charge to the jury was eminently fair and impartial. It was lengthy and painstaking, covering every point of the law."

Even in the face of certain knowledge that jury deliberations would not be forthcoming until after 10:00 AM on Friday December 23, scores of people remained all night around the criminal court building hoping to be the first to hear the verdict in the case of Nan Patterson. A rumor reported herein that the jury vote stood at 11 to one for acquittal. A little after 12 noon the jury reported itself to be hopelessly deadlocked and then Justice Davis dismissed them. As the foreman left the courtroom he stated that the vote in the case stood at six for conviction and six for acquittal. However he would not state what specific charge or charges the six in favor of conviction voted for. According to the foreman only one ballot was taken. It was then found that there was such a vast difference of opinion that the remainder of the time was taken up in argument. A little later it was reported, unofficially, that the six who voted for conviction broke down as follows; one for murder in the second degree; two for manslaughter in the first degree; and three for manslaughter in the second degree.

In a lengthy recap of the case, after the jury was dismissed one journalist remarked; "Nan Patterson, or Randolph, is a particularly beautiful woman. She came west as one of the 'Pretty Maidens' in the first *Floradora* company that visited San Francisco. There she met Young and he became infatuated with her. On more than one occasion he left his wife and home to be with the Patterson woman and once he announced that he had gone with her finally. His friends managed to get him back and after a wild time in Los Angeles he returned to his wife who forgave him." In continuing the story the reporter said; "It was thought that a trip to Europe might break him from the girl and he was booked to sail with his wife from New York. Nan Patterson was also in New York and on the very morning that the ship was to sail Young left his wife saying that he wanted to buy a hat and would meet her on the dock. He joined the Patterson woman and the two were driving down Broadway in a hack when Young was shot. Nan Patterson was arrested and charged with murder, but her claim is that Young shot himself after telling her that he could not face life without her. A determined attempt is being made to fix the crime on her."

One editorial comment on the outcome of the trial noted that it had been said in court by the lawyers that morality was not at issue in trial. But as far as this editor was concerned, it was; "The record of the year from the footlights to the prison cell as it was brought out in the full and particular story of nocturnal revelry, loose marital relations and sensual pleasure-seeking, culminating in sudden death and a murder charge, was one in which there was contained a moral issue not subordinate in importance even to the question of fact as to how Caesar Young came to his death.

According to one account, after Nan was taken back to the Tombs after the verdict was in; "after the jury announced that it was unable to agree in her case, she had an attack of hysteria during which she was so violent that it took several men to restrain her." Also, according to the story; "The girl completely lost her had and smashed around the prison, vowing that she would not remain there another minute. She raved about the jury which had failed to acquit her and about Assistant District Attorney Rand, who prosecuted her and several times her violence became so serious that it was feared she would do herself an injury. Eventually her strength gave out and she sank to the floor a limp, spiritless mass." And then; "She was taken to a cell, where she huddled herself up in a corner and refused to speak to or even look at anybody. The girl is completely crushed and a physician has been assigned to watch her closely." All of that hyperbole was, of course, nonsense and complete fabrication. The next paragraph in this account noted that Levy and O'Reilly visited her at the Tombs that same afternoon and she calmly asked about bail, another trial, and so forth.

A closer approximation to Nan's post-verdict condition was perhaps found in the following account. When the jury reported itself hung and was discharged, wrote a newsman, she turned to her father and threw herself sobbing on his shoulder. She fainted, was revived and was led out back to the Tombs "sobbing violently."

Levy announced that if a third trial was to occur, he would immediately ask for bail and have the bail amount reduced to $15,000. Crowd reaction was so intense that, said a newsman; "the crowds which were outside the courtroom all the morning pursued foreman Harmer of the jury when he left the court after the final adjournment. He boarded a trolley, but men chased the car to his business office and mounted police were called upon to dispense the throng." With respect to Patterson's financial condition, Levy stated; "The defendant is wholly without means. When counsel assured the defense of her case it was with the understanding and in the expectation that the defendant would be sufficiently equipped with means, if not to properly compensate them, at least to meet the disbursements and actual expenses which were bound to arise. This she has never been able to do, so that during the progress of the trial we did not even have the stenographer's minutes of the testimony, but were obliged to depend upon our own notes as to proofs given through a trial spreading over three weeks."

In a recap of the trial from a west coast newspaper the journalist called the crime "one of the most sensational in New York criminal annals. Its peculiar circumstances, the prominence of Caesar Young in sporting circles and the glamour thrown around the central figure in the case because of her membership in one of the famous *Floradora* companies, all tended to lend it an interest hardly rivaled in recent years...the proceedings of the trial have been read from coast to coast and have held a place on the first page of the metropolitan press." He continued his account by noting the cab driver Michaels testified he heard a shot but knew nothing else; "Then a flood of witnesses turned up. Their stories, however, could not stand investigation and one after another the witnesses were cast aside as sensation seekers." Concluding his piece he stated; "and no case in years, surrounded as it was at first with so much seeming mystery, has been so barren of the dramatic and unexpected in the court room."

Speculation on the day before Christmas was that juror number nine, G. W. Yeandle, could have been the problem, because; "It was Mr. Yeandle who had put some of the most telling questions to witnesses...[At that time jurors could question witnesses who were on the stand, through the sitting judge]. In the jury room he was said to have been the advocate of Nan's cause, arguing most strenuously on her behalf. [See chapter 9, footnote #56 paragraph for an interesting later involvement of Yeandle in an unrelated case]. It was also said that in the jury room it was obvious that nobody would ever be won over to the other side – that the six for acquittal would always be for acquittal and the six in favor of conviction would always be in favor of conviction.

On that day before Christmas, Nan spent the time in her cell, as usual. The suitcase she had packed with her belongings and toiletries, in anticipation of going home at the end of trial number 2, was opened and unpacked. On that same day District Attorney Jerome announced that he would not agree to a reduction of his prisoner's bail, from $20,000, and that meant Nan would not be going home for Christmas. In the past she had been unable to raise $20,000 and she had no prospect of doing so then. While Jerome had the option to not retry Nan, everything pointed towards a third trial being held. Nan's lawyer Daniel O'Reilly urged a speedy retrial claiming that some new evidence had come to light that the defense considered important. Some .32 caliber bullets had been found in Young's truck, that is, in the possession of a man who had never owned or carried a gun. On that June 4 day all the Youngs' luggage sailed off to Europe, minus the Youngs. It came back to the United States when the liner Germanic made its return voyage to New York City, from England. It was when that luggage was searched when it returned to New York that the bullets were found. It was a .32 caliber bullet that killed Caesar Young. Assistant District Attorney Rand admitted to the finding of the ammunition but contended those bullets belonged to Margaret Young. Thus, trial number two was at an end.

A series of photographs showing Nan and her expressions during trial #2.

CHAPTER 6. AFTER TRIAL #2.

The time after trial number two and before the start of trial number three was mostly about trying to get Ann Elizabeth Patterson released on bail, or even on her own recognizance. It was also about the state delaying the start of trial number three until it was literally forced to by a court order. Finally, it was much ado about the Smiths, as they finally surfaced and increasingly became more and more important to the case and its outcome. Nan remained in the public interest and a brief report near the end of 1904 had it that Nan was taking notes about her prison experiences and was expected to write a book about those experiences.

The move to get Patterson out of her cell was mostly focused on bail conditions but other methods also were mentioned, such as was apparently attempted in Ohio. Near the end of 1904 it was reported that Cleveland people who believed Nan was innocent had the opportunity of signing a petition to that effect, which was to be presented to District Attorney William Jerome. The petition asked that the murder indictment be dismissed and that Nan be set free. Originator of the petition was Mrs. F. G. Stone of Cleveland. Reportedly, Stone did not know Patterson or any of her relatives or anyone else connected with the case and that her efforts in the situation were purely humanitarian. That petition was put into circulation on December 25 and as of the 26th had 50 signatures. Stone was confident that at least 50,000 residents of Cleveland would sign it if it could be placed before them. The petition was worded as follows; "We, the undersigned resident of Cleveland, believing in the innocence of Miss Nan Patterson, do respectfully ask you to petition the honorable court for a cancellation of the indictment against the young woman."

According to one account just a few days after the jury was dismissed telegrams had been received by Nan from Wheeling West Virginia announcing that four "prominent" men in that city were prepared to furnish bail for her in any amount up to $50,000. Patterson would not reveal the names of the men but a newsman declared they were; Charles W. Swisher, secretary of state-elect; H. J. Price, merchant; T. E. Deveney, a hotel keeper; and Howard Black, a banker; all from Fairmont West Virginia. Shortly after, T. A. Deveney described as one of the wealthiest men in Fairmont confirmed that he, Price and Edward Slack (the latter two called local business men) would furnish bail to the extent of $50,000 if necessary "not in order to receive notoriety, but because they believe her innocent of the crime with which she is charged." A telegram sent to Nan at the Tombs bore the names of the latter three named plus that of C. W. Swisher. However, Swisher came forward to state he never signed the telegram nor authorized his name in any way to be used in that connection. Around the same time an announcement from District Attorney Jerome's office declared that Nan would not be retried "for at least two months."

More information about the length of the delay before a retrial came soon thereafter. One newsman even speculated that there was every reason to believe Nan would not face the ordeal of another trial for several months at least, if ever. That there would be no trial for at least several months became apparent when it was learned that John Millin, former partner of Young and one of the witnesses for the prosecution obtained permission from Rand to return to Sacramento California in order to take care of his business interests. Millin stated he would be detained in Sacramento on business for at least three months. Rand's office declared it to be impossible for the case to proceed without Millin as a witness.

Abraham Levy had a meeting with Rand around the same time and was assured there was no prospect of a trial in the near future. It was also revealed by people in the office of District Attorney Jerome that the state would not incur the expense of another trial unless some trace could be found of the missing J. Morgan Smith and his wife It was said to be Rand's belief that without Smith on hand to be a witness, or to be identified by pawnbroker Stern, no conviction could ever be secured.

Patterson was said to have received many letters of sympathy in the mail, more than 200 in total, from all parts of America and some of them reportedly contained money. Meanwhile the offer of bail that had supposedly emanated from four men in Fairmont West Virginia proved to be "without foundation." Besides the false signature from Swisher on the document it was discovered that two others involved "were not in positions to raise the required sum."

One of the well-known and popular actors of the day was May Irwin. According to an announcement from Nan's lawyers, Irwin had offered to furnish up to $50,000 for the release of Patterson from the Tombs. Irwin was said to have personally called at the Tombs, on December 30, and left a letter addressed to Nan and the announcement that she was willing to furnish up to $50,000 in bail was made just a few minutes after the Irwin left the jail. Meanwhile, another of the attention-seeking "eye-witnesses" who supposedly saw Young fire the shot that killed him surfaced around this time. That man was W. B. Meyers, described herein as a wealthy naval stores dealer in Jacksonville Florida. Judge H. D. D. Twiggs of Savannah Georgia wrote a letter to Nan's counsel conveying the information that Meyers saw Young fire the shot. He should not be confused with Algernon C. Meyer of Deland Florida. According to the story from Savannah W. B. Meyers first made known the fact that he saw the shooting a few days after the event occurred. He mentioned this "casually" then to his Savannah lawyer while conducting other business. Then he later told the story to Twiggs and declared his intention to send his name to Nan and to go to New York City to testify. During the trial Twiggs followed the proceedings waiting for the testimony of Meyers and was greatly surprised when it was not used. He concluded that Meyers never wrote to Nan so Twiggs did so himself. In this account speculation was that Meyers was the man Hazelton claimed was beside him on the day that he, Hazelton, saw the shooting.

On December 31 District Attorney Jerome announced that Nan Patterson would be tried again and that she would not be admitted to bail, regardless of the amount. While the second trial was being arranged the defendant would remain a prisoner in the Tombs. Said Jerome; "You can state officially that no bail will be accepted for the woman and that she will be put on trial again." At this time that earlier bail "offer" made by Thomas Deveney, Edward Slack and H. J. Price of West Virginia "is now said to have been sent in a spirit of fun." Pending the second trial investigators from Jerome's office were "scouring the country" in an effort to find the elusive Smiths. Jerome was said to believe that finding the Smiths would materially strengthen his case.

When Nan heard the news about no bail being allowed and that a retrial would definitely take place she was reported to have said; "I have been friendless for so long that I cannot understand why, when people offer bail for me as high as $50,000. Mr. Jerome insists on persecuting me by keeping me in prison. What object would I have in running away, and where would I go to?" She added; "My future lies in New York, where I expect to live and work and help support my parents, who have sacrificed what money they have saved for the costs of my trial and the few necessities which I feel I have to have, but which the prison authorities do no furnish free." And, she continued; "I have spent all of my own money since I was first locked up, and I am obliged to look to my father for the small outlays absolutely necessary here. Rest assured, however, that I shall pay him back in good time."

The story about the two men, each named Meyers who "saw" the shooting got more confused as the year 1905 began. Following the published statement that W. B. Meyers saw the shooting "and Meyers denial and assertion that he was never in New York, it now develops that Algernon C. Meyers was in New York at the time and saw the shooting and that he has given his testimony to District Attorney Jerome." [The similarities were a little forced and exaggerated since the name of the first man was Meyer, but there were similarities]. Soon after the shooting it was reported that Algernon Meyers witnessed the affair and at the time an attempt was made to confirm the story. It could not be done in New York because Meyers had left that city. It could not be confirmed in Jacksonville for the reason that Meyers' whereabouts were not known to his mother, who lived in Jacksonville while Algernon was living in Deland Florida. That story was dropped without further investigation until the story of W. B. Meyers alleged connection with the case developed a few days earlier. It was then that Algernon was located and he was asked about the matter. Said Algernon; "I was in New York, witnessed the shooting, testified before Jerome, my testimony being about the same as Nan Patterson's." Algernon, it was speculated, was the man Hazelton claimed was standing beside him. Reportedly, there was no relation between Algernon Meyers and W. B. Meyers. It was also reported that lawyers for Patterson had been unable to locate "this important witness" for the defense.

The hunt for J. Morgan Smith and his wife continued all during this time with, apparently, no success. More and more J. Morgan Smith was being forced into the case and reporters fled that story with one writing that; "the prosecution claims that it was Smith who forced Miss Patterson to kill young."

At the very beginning of 1905 John D. Millin, the business partner of Caesar Young, when asked if he still believed Nan killed Young, said; "I am confident of the fact as I am that I have a nose on my face....Police officials and those who have followed the case closely from the outset are of the same opinion." When he spoke those words Millin was in Los Angeles looking after his business interests. He was a partner with Young for some 10 years. Because he took the stand and testified against Patterson, he said; "I have received at least a thousand letters from her admirers all over the country. Many of them were anonymous, some of them contained threats; I tore all of them up and threw them into the waste basket." He added; "Perhaps I am biased in my opinion but I know the woman so well and what had transpired between her and Young that I cannot see the case in any other light than that she is guilty of the crime with which she is charged...Young told me on several occasions of the threats that she had made against his life and he was afraid of her all the time. He told me the day before he was shot that he was fearful that she could do him harm..." According to Millin Young first met Nan on the way from San Francisco to Los Angeles, by train, in October 1902 and was with her a great deal after they arrived in Los Angeles. Finally Young wanted to get rid of her and he gave her $800 to get her out of Los Angeles. From there she went to New York and then returned to Los Angeles in the spring of 1904. She followed Young wherever he want. When Millin left Los Angeles in the spring of 1904 Young was still with her. Then she went on to New York where later in the season Young joined her. Millin insisted Young never carried a revolver in his life. Concluded Millin; "I think by this time the world knows pretty well what kind of a woman Nan Patterson is, although the newspapers have been unfair to the prosecution in their attempts to weave a halo about the woman's head She does not deserve it. If she could be known as I know her there would be little sympathy felt for her."

Also at the very beginning of 1905 there appeared a lengthy article about Ann Elizabeth Patterson giving readers glimpses into her career, her background, her trial and, of course, a moral lesson. The article occupied about half a page, was reprinted in many different papers and was called "The Primrose Path." That came from William Shakespeare's *Hamlet*, "primrose path of dalliance." It was about the pleasant route through life, of enjoyment and dissipation while being a rejection of the difficult and arduous path of righteousness through life, a path that lead to Heaven, in favor of the easier path to sin. Subheads of the piece included; "Nan Patterson has followed it [primrose path] to the prison bars;" and "Whether innocent or guilty of murder she is paying the penalty of a life of so-called pleasure." And, wrote the unnamed author; "Attracted by the glare of the footlights she forsakes family and friends for the tinsel of the stage – a moral in her tragedy." The piece began by remarking; "From the glare of the footlights to the gloom of a cell in the Tombs" would be a fitting title of a story of the life of Nan. From that stage life "to be branded as a murderer by thousands and to hear the bitter and cutting words of the stern prosecutor as he laid bare the secrets of her past life." Such was the experience of Nan "and it has turned her from a beautiful and care-free girl to a prematurely aged woman." Nan Randolph Patterson was quite well known along Broadway among theatrical people for several years before she so suddenly took the center of the stage; "Among the profession though it was simply Nan Randolph."

According to the story detailed in "The Primrose Path" [most of it wrong] Nan was born in Washington D. C., the daughter of a minister and was raised amid the religious surroundings of a Christian home. And because she had "Always a wild and willful disposition, the simple life did not appeal to her." It was agreed herein that she was an "uncommonly beautiful" child and the praise called forth by her good looks as she grew older, turned her thoughts in directions wholly opposed to that intended for her by her parents, and before she was many years in her teens she went to New York and obtained a place in the chorus." Stage life "caused her to forget the religious training she had received" and she decided to become a great actress." Nan found that; "Fine clothes and a 'good time' were to her liking." The reader was told that; "She was handsome in face and form and it was not long before young scions of wealthy families and elderly men of means who haunt the 'bald head' row began to haunt the stage door and make her acquaintance." The flowers and champagne suppers they furnished were also not amiss, "jewels and gems were showered on her and more than one, smitten with her beauty, laid their hearts at her feet and begged her hand in marriage. But she refused them all and finally married a young man in the profession name of Martin." Continuing on the journalist observed; "The confining bonds of matrimony were evidently not to her liking and when *Floradora* was imported she applied for and got a position in the front row." When the company set off for California it was a fateful trip for it was on that journey that she met Frank Thomas Young.

With respect to that initial meeting, the author of "The Primrose Path" remarked; "Although a married man he immediately fell a victim to the charms of the beautiful and vivacious show girl." Upon their arrival in San Francisco he installed her in an apartment in Oakland and Young began to lead a dual existence, at least with regard to the women in his life. While there on the west coast Nan, according to this account, sued her husband for a divorce and also deserted the stage. Margaret Young found out about her husband's double life and, according to Millin, Young repeatedly tried to sever his "unholy relations" with the chorus girl, but his infatuation was too strong or his will power too weak for she never succeeded. "Nan Patterson's beauty has been the cause of other troubles in which lives have been forfeited. An actor in another play who had proposed to her became insane over her refusal and committed suicide in her presence. Another admirer of hers killed himself on the coast." Nan remained with Young until the spring of 1904 at which time they returned east, in March 1904, for the first time since their meeting. During all this time Caesar tried to hide his relations with Nan from his wife. His friends and relatives pleaded with him to give her up and finally induced him to agree to take a trip to Europe. After a recap of June 3 and June 4 this piece concluded by saying; "Although one young and wayward girl has dearly paid the price for her folly the case has served to point a moral to others that the snares and pitfalls of the innocent maiden behind the footlights are many, and more than one, unable to stand the temptation offered, has partaken of the fatal apple." And; "In conclusion, the Primrose Path means a life of pleasure, of ease and gaiety, strewn with roses red, but to Nan Patterson the glamour has been removed, and it is streaked with the life blood of Caesar Young."

On January 4 Nan appeared in the New York State Supreme Court before Justice Greenbaum when her lawyers argued on behalf of bail being granted to their client. Pointed out to Greenbaum was the long period of incarceration to that date, that the District Attorney would not fix a time for the retrial, even though counsel for Patterson had appealed to Jerome to set a date. Levy also said his client was ready to furnish bail in any amount. Assistant district Attorney Rand was also in court and argued that the application for bail should be denied. Greenbaum reserved his decision.

On the following morning proceedings before Greenbaum were delayed because Rand had not filed paperwork that was necessary and which he had been expected to have already done. Thus proceedings on the bail application had to be postponed until the afternoon. Lawyer Abraham Levy walked over to Rand's office to jog his memory and to remind him of his duty to file the paperwork. That caused a reporter to assert; "It is plain that the district attorney's office is not interested in the efforts of Nan Patterson to get out of the Tombs." Later, on January 6, Nan Patterson was denied bail.

In denying the application for bail Justice Greenbaum declared that counsel for Nan "made no effort to convince the court that there is improbability of securing a conviction at a second trial unless the disagreement of the jury in the first trial would justify such an inference." That, however, did not appear sufficient to him as it was a matter of not infrequent occurrence that juries failed to agree in cases which, upon a subsequent trial upon the some statements of fact, a conclusion was speedily reached by another jury.

A report published in a San Francisco newspaper at the end of January declared, in its first words; "J. Morgan Smith was in town." The report added that; "It was Smith's pistol with which the murder of Young was supposed to have been committed" and it was for that reason that he had been so relentlessly sought after. [Note that herein it said the pistol belonged to Smith, even though it had never been tied to him and no evidence existed to reinforce such a statement]. Apparently, the story began when someone on the Bowery in New York told someone else that Smith had reached the Pacific Coast and that he had wired to a friend, "I am in Frisco." Added a reporter; "This was true, for day before yesterday the much sought after witness was parading Market Street and later made his headquarters at 543 O'Farrell Street, where he is acquainted with a couple of actor folks." Smith was then reported to have left San Francisco on January 26 but was expected back in that city on January 28. According to this tale, Young was in San Francisco to "look up evidence" that might be of some advantage to his sister-in-law and that naturally he did not wish to give the New York prosecutors anything regarding the pistol – or anything else – that might strengthen the case against Nan. Smith was said to be widely known in San Francisco; he had been to that city often; and about two years earlier he was a familiar figure in the downtown district. He left this city to follow the races on the Eastern circuit. When he fled New York City, a few days after the death of Young, he went to the Middle West and then to Los Angeles and then to San Francisco, at least according to this story. Smith told friends that he knew nothing about the pistol.

Another lengthy article and interview with Nan Patterson was published in the middle of February 1905. It was conducted with an unnamed female reporter with the *Sun* (NY) newspaper who began her piece by commenting that; "She seems to a woman interviewer like a butterfly in strange quarters." Unlike most of the so-called interviews with Nan, this one probably did take place and the quotes were likely to be more or less accurate. Many of the preceding "interviews" never took place at all, despite the supposed quotations attributed to the prisoner. This one took place with the approval, and under the supervision of, the detainee's counsel. The lawyers had earlier told their client to not talk to the press. The reporter who wrote this piece explained that it was not easy to get to see and interview Nan as this journalist went through "a forest of thorn-like objections" from her lawyer Abraham Levy who put the reporter through "a sort of third degree" as to every particular about the proposed interview. In her description of her subject the reporter said; "She is really of medium height, 5 feet 5, but she seems shorter and her natural slenderness is accentuated. She is dressed all in brown, a short skirt tightly fitting. She runs once during the interview across the corridor to overtake some one and you notice her fleetness and grace." And, added the journalist; "She has small features, small ears, a small nose, a small mouth which discloses perfectly regular white teeth. Underneath her gray eyes are dark circles and the face has the creamy pallor of prison life.

At that point in the interview attorney Levy, who remained near his client throughout the interview, reminded Nan that she was not to talk about her case. "The eyes are fixed obediently on Mr. Levy's face. You would say that Nan Patterson was temperamentally obedient. There are women like that even in these days; women who are amiably weak, amiably obedient, who naturally obey the tone of any one who speaks to them with authority. Her expression is the passive one of a girl who is accustomed to be told what she should do, and if she does not intend to do it would not think of expressing her revolt in any flagrant word or deed that might offend." The pair conducted the interview sitting on the hard orison bench with Levy hovering discreetly in the near distance. Patterson was asked about her thoughts. "Thoughts? I try not to think. I'm tired of thinking." Then she was asked how she spent her time in the Tombs. "I read some. They let us play solitaire sometimes, and (with a slight shudder) sometimes I talk with the other women here." She explained that what she read most were magazines, magazines of short stories. She had, she said, read only one or two books in her eight months of incarceration. Said the reporter; "Little stories, little games, little talks. Perhaps that trio of littleness expresses the present life of such a woman as well as a longer description might do. They are the resources of an immature underdeveloped mind, of one who has lived always on the surface." Nan told the journalist that she read the letters she received, from all over the country, and she had about 5,000; "Some of the women [who wrote those letters] have been hard on me, but the greater part are very nice."

The reporter thought, at one point, that Nan may have been on the verge of uttering some kind of complaint about the prison system, but a warning look from Levy checked her. Said Nan; "Nothing. I have no complaint to make. Every one has been so kind. Warden Flynn would do more for me if he could, but there is so much jealousy among the other women that he has to be very careful not to show any favor. Mrs. O'Brien, the matron, is good to us all Once in a while she lets me go to the door with her and look out." [That is, look out into an interior, but open, courtyard – she was never allowed to go outside]. Asked about exercise and food, Patterson replied; "I walk up and down the corridor in the daytime. That is the exercise. The food? Yes, it is all right." Then the interviewer asked her about the evenings. "Evenings! There are no evenings. I am locked in every afternoon at 4 o'clock, right after supper, and stay there until 8 o'clock the next morning. I have been very ill with a bad cold the last few days and I have been allowed to stay in bed to 10 o'clock." Nan was allowed to show the reporter her cell. There were two tiers of cells in the women's section; she was housed in cell #21 on the upper tier. The cell was large enough to hold a narrow iron bed from which, without stretching out the arm, a person could touch the wall on the free side. There was a little more space, perhaps 6 inches at the foot of the bed where the water from a simple faucet dripped into a wooden paid. Finally, Nan was asked if she would go back on the stage. "Never. I have had enough of notoriety, enough of the stage, enough of everything. I want to get away somewhere, anywhere." Concluded the interviewing journalist; "The last look at Nan Patterson recalls to the interviewer a boat on a summer sea. Following it, undaunted, a butterfly, shaken loose from the sail at the starting, mile after mile, seeking shelter and safety."

Habeas corpus proceedings on behalf of Nan were launched at the end of February, in another effort to free the woman from detention. On February 28 those proceedings, held before Justice Gaynor, in the Brooklyn Supreme Court, were adjourned for one day when a motion to adjoin was made by Assistant District Attorney Johnson who asked for adjournment in order that Rand might be present; Rand was involved in another case at the same time. Gaynor, after noting the crowds in the court-room that had gathered to catch a glimpse of the prisoner, said to counsel Abraham Levy; "Don't bring her here tomorrow unless there is some necessity. I don't want such a following like this today. The writ of certiorari will be all that is necessary." According to this account Nan was brought to the Brooklyn courthouse from the Tombs in a cab, by Warden Flynn. It was only the second time that she had been out of the Tombs or the courtroom since her incarceration on June 4. [The Tombs and the courthouse were directly across the street from each other and connected with an enclosed overpass known as the "Bridge of Sighs." Thus, Nan did not go outside going back and forth between the New York courtroom and her cell in the Tombs]. Reportedly, during that cab ride she took a "keen delight" in looking out of the cab window on that trip.

Another account of the same event – the trip to the Brooklyn courthouse – wrote of it differently. In this tale Nan walked from the Tombs to the Brooklyn Bridge entrance [about half of a mile away]. "Without assistance she jumped aboard a Green and Gates Avenue trolley car, followed by Warden Flynn and a deputy sheriff." Her walking progress to the bridge attracted an ever increasing crowd. Carrying the flamboyant lies even further the account declared that for that trip she wore a blue tailor-made gown that she made herself. The above account stated she wore a black dress for the trip, the same one she had worn every day of the trial. In fact, she had only one "outdoor" garment, that black dress. She did no sewing in the Tombs. When the trolley that Nan had boarded arrived opposite the Brooklyn Court House [another half mile or so] "a crowd of several hundred men and women were awaiting the arrival of the actress. And that courtroom in Brooklyn was so packed that; "Court officers had to literally drag several spectators from their seats to make room for Miss Patterson and her father."

An editorial on Patterson's latest attempt to win bail stated that; "The request is not unreasonable." The editor added; "Without prejudice the statement may be made that belief in her guilt has been dispelled largely through the conduct of the prosecution In the first place it deferred the test as many months as possible, and more months than should have been devoted to delay, and then, when it presented its case the public was astounded in view of the evidence that there should have been disagreement instead of a quick verdict of acquittal." Concluded the newsman; "The trial was long ago. There has been ample time since for another but no movement to bring another about. If the prosecution realizes that it cannot convict, the present detention of the prisoner, while insistently demanding to be arraigned, is a wrong to the prisoner, and in any event it is a wrong to the public."

The prisoner's lawyers were back in court on March 1 to argue for bail. Levy argued Nan was suffering from general debility and in view of her long confinement in the Tombs she should be accorded either an immediate trial or be admitted to a reasonable amount of bail. In opposing the application Rand claimed that Nan would be given a trial as soon as was possible, but it would be unfair to other prisoners in the Tombs charged with homicide to give this woman any preference and privilege. Rand said it was likely she would be brought to trial in April. Levy then replied that if Rand would promise to bring her to trial in April then he would withdraw his bail application. However, Rand answered that the District Attorney's office, in fairness, could not make such a promise. At that point the hearing ended with Justice Gaynor reserving his decision.

On March 4 Justice Gaynor issued his ruling on the matter. He ordered that Nan Patterson had to be place on trial by May 1, 1905, or be released on bail. In hi decision he said; "The woman is, of course, entitled to a speedy trial. She has been tried, the jury disagreeing 6 to 6. It seems doubtful if the District Attorney moves her trial again. Unless he does so before May 1, let her be discharged on bail."

Another lengthy interview with the prisoner appeared in print on March 6, in the *World* (NY). That paper was part of the William Randolph Hearst chain and very much prone to manufacture material out of the air, not just to attribute quotes that had not taken place but to invent the entire interview itself. How much of this so-called interview was accurate was anybody's guess. It began realistically by noting that Nan received her reporter visitor (male) at the Tombs only after a promise had been exacted from him, by her counsel, that he would ask no questions about her case. He began his article with a description; "As she rested herself on one of the benches just outside her cell it was noticeable that she had gained in health since her first trial in December. Her figure was more plump and there was a suggestion of color in her cheeks seldom seen in a prisoner who has spent nine weary months in close confinement." One of the first questions he asked her was about a report that she was to wed a wealthy man as soon as she left the Tombs. Replied Nan; "I expect never to marry. I have no wealthy admirer waiting to lead me to the altar as soon as I come out of prison. I am not even engaged. There is no longer any man, rich or poor, in my case, and I do not think there ever will be. As soon as I am free I shall leave New York, go to the West...and devote the rest of my life to doing all the good I am."

Moving on to another topic, Patterson declared; "I tell you, there's no such thing as justice in New York. My, but I never want to see the city again once I am free. A man or woman with plenty of money can do just as they please here, but what does the poor girl or man get? Nothing. By the time of the interview she knew about Gaynor's decision to try her by May 1 and was pleased; "Do you know that some of the visitors whom the guides show through the prison treat me as if I were some kind of an animal on exhibition. When I hear them coming I run to

my cell in self-defense. Then they stand at the end of the corridor and shout: 'Miss Patterson, why don't you come out and
let us see you?'" Nan was also asked if she would return to the
stage. "No, indeed. I have had all the stage I want...It's all very
nice to talk about the glamour of the footlights and all that, but
I tell you – and you can take my word for it – that it's a hard life
for those who are in it." With respect to prison life Patterson
said; "It's true that I do not eat the regular prison fare. I have
my meals served to me by the caterer, and all the prison people,
from the Warden down, are very kind to me But they don't treat
me any differently from any other prisoner. I have no privileges.
Any one who can pay for them can have meals sent them by the
caterer." She explained that her father paid for them.

Another editorial on the plight of the detainee came in the
middle of March. It became by recalling the time Nan had
taken the stand to testify during trial number two, and refer-
enced Rand's cross examination of the witness. "For one entire
day one of the keenest legal minds of the New York bar tried to
catch this young woman of 22 in some of her statements. He
probed mercilessly into her life history. The inquisition was
the keenest torture. When the cross-examination was ended
the woman was on the verge of nervous prostration But there
was never a lapse in all the mass of testimony. The lawyers
failed to extort a single utterance that could be used against the
witness. The cross-questioner gave up in despair. To the very
last Nan Patterson smiled and kept the even tenor of her way."
The editor observed that lawyers did not usually advise one accused of a crime to take the stand but; "She invaded the enemy's
country alone and undaunted." However, even if this editor
believed her innocent of murder she was guilty in other ways;
"It is difficult to believe that she killed Caesar Young. The presumption is against such belief. Indirectly, however, she caused
the man's death. Handicapped by a keen remorse, her guilty life
made an open book, scorned by her sex, this girl stood at bay
and using every power of mind and heart, fought for her life.

Rand had been prone in the past to making outrageous statements as to what he would soon prove in a court of law. Some such pronouncements were made in the courtroom, in opening remarks and some of them were made outside of the courtroom. Taking perhaps a page from that book, one of Nan's lawyers, Daniel O'Reilly, declared in a press conference toward the end of March that the defense would be able to prove the following facts, not brought out at trials one or two. One point was that Young was the owner of a 32-caliber revolver; second point was that he had such a revolver in his possession on June 3 while at the racetrack; third point was that on the afternoon of June 3 Young took a pistol away from his wife Margaret; fourth point was that Margaret owned a 32-caliber revolver; fifth point was that in Caesar's trunk, sent to England on the morning of June 4 on the liner Germanic, was found a "large number" of 32-caliber revolver cartridges. It was a 32-caliber bullet that killed Young. O'Reilly declared; "If Nan Patterson is every placed on trial again, and I have very serious doubts that she will we shall be able to prove, even to the satisfaction of Mr. Rand...that Young committed suicide and Nan never had the pistol in her possession." O'Reilly claimed to have two witnesses who had seen him with a revolver on June 3 at the track and he had four witnesses who saw Nan and the Smiths take the last train from the track on June 3, which made it impossible for J. Morgan Smith to have purchased the weapon earlier that afternoon. O'Reilly and the other lawyers on Patterson's side never proved any of these points, except for point five, for which they already had evidence in hand. However, for reasons never explained it was never introduced in court as evidence. They had the affidavit of United States Customs House Inspector Arthur J. Scanlan to prove the presence of the cartridges in Young's trunk. That trunk went to England by itself and returned to America on the Germanic's return crossing. When it arrived back in America Scanlan examined the trunk [in New York City] and found the cartridges.

By far the biggest development in this case in the period between trial number two and trial number three was the announcement that came on the afternoon of Thursday, March 30; after being on the run for nearly 10 months, J. Morgan Smith and his wife Julia were arrested in Cincinnati Ohio. While the prosecution had long insisted that Smith had bought the murder weapon that prosecution had never advanced any reason or logic as to why the Smiths would have been involved. That is, there was no motive in sight. Some of the bizarre thinking behind Rand and company was revealed in this account. It was noted that the couple were wanted as witnesses in the Patterson trial but now, said the journalist; "they will have to stand trial themselves on the charge that they conspired to extort money from bookmaker Caesar Young on the pretense that Nan was about to become a mother and was in need of support." It was expected that the pair would be quickly extradited from Ohio and they were expected to be back in New York City for trial number three, then tentatively slated to start April 10.

Detectives pursuing the couple were said to have been close to catching them for some time and on Tuesday, March 28 had what they deemed reliable information that the Smiths would be in Cincinnati on Thursday March 30; "So yesterday Assistant District Attorney Rand had before the Grand Jury Mrs. Margaret Young, William D. Luce [Young's brother-in-law] Joseph Hewitt [the newsboy who "saw" Nan and Morgan arguing on the night of June 3] and several policemen who had been connected with the case; "It didn't take long to hear the testimony and draw the indictments." Then DA Jerome sent a dispatch to Cincinnati Police Chief Milliken; "Arrest and hold for extradition J. Morgan Smith, wanted in New York on a charge of criminal conspiracy. Smith will be found at the Grand Hotel, Fourth Street, Cincinnati." Soon a message from Cincinnati arrived that the pair had been arrested. Rand immediately got New York State Governor Higgins on the phone and explained the need for extradition. Within half an hour New York Police Department Detective Sergeant McNaught started for Albany to pick up the paperwork. From there he was to go straight to Cincinnati, expected there on the Saturday. It was confidently felt that the Smiths would be in New York City on Monday, April 3.

One of the odder things about the saga of the Smiths was that the reports of their wanderings over the past half year or so indicated that the state knew where they were almost all of that time. According to this account, a private detective agency was employed some five months earlier with the result that the couple were tracked to Canada; "Since then the detectives have never lost sight of either of the Smiths for long." [Since that implied the state knew the whereabouts of them since sometime in October why were they not arrested and extradited to New York for trials one and two?]. Smith and his wife roamed all over Canada; at various times they had been reported to the District Attorney's office as being in Montreal, Quebec City, Toronto and Hamilton. Then they left Canada and crossed back into the United States. During their travels they used several different names, including Adams, Bishop and Collins. Frequently the Smiths separated, to meet again in some other city. In the United States four detectives followed one or the other or both of them to Detroit, Cleveland, Pittsburgh, and Covington Kentucky, wherein Julia Smith had relatives. On Monday March 27 Julia Smith, under the name of Mrs. W. A. Adams, was at the Hollenden Hotel in Cleveland. Smith was in Pittsburgh. Detectives learned the Smiths had arranged to meet up in Cincinnati on March 30. One item wondered about by the District Attorney's office was where the couple got the money they must have needed for all that traveling. Smith reportedly had no distinct means of support. All through the trial Rand had tried to use Morgan as a point to connect Nan with the murder. He tried to show, or imply, Morgan bought the murder weapon on the afternoon of June 3 from pawnbroker Stern. Perhaps, though, the presence of the Smiths at the trial would work to Nan's advantage since the state had no evidence tying Morgan to the purchase of the gun, it was all groundless allegations from Rand. If that was the case it could have explained why Rand never had the pair arrested and extradited for the trials that were then completed. Also, it gave Rand time to concoct the very ridiculous story about extortion and conspiracy. It allowed a motive, however strange and fanciful, to surface and to implicate the Smiths. That conspiracy indictment reportedly was based on a letter written by Mrs. Smith to Caesar Young. She asked Young to see her at once. It read; "Nan has been with me since Monday, when she left mother, accompanied by my sister May Queen, who fearing, in her perturbed condition, that she might do something either serious to you or to herself, came to New York. I should very much like to get the whole thing straightened out, and understand what is what. I understand what the matter is and want you to do what is right at once...You must come and see me and get the whole matter straightened out." In Cincinnati the Smiths were registered at the Grand Hotel as Mr. and Mrs. H. H. Banning of New York, when they were arrested.

It was reported herein that the Smiths were shadowed all over Canada for months by T. H. Aiken of Montreal, who worked for the Thiel Detective Agency, and by S. P. Ward of New York, representing District Attorney Jerome. When the Smiths arrived in Cincinnati they were in need of money and therefore called at the nearby home of Frank Queen of Covington Kentucky (a relative of Julia). Reportedly, Queen and his wife, prominent in their area, declined to receive the Smiths in their home, denied them any financial help and repudiated them as relatives. Said a journalist; "Detectives Aiken and Ward have been in touch with the Smiths for a long time and even accompanied them on pleasure trips" during their time on the run. When Morgan was searched at Cincinnati police headquarters after being arrested he had on his person a "cheap watch" and $2.85 in cash in his pockets.

A different report on the arrest of the Smiths mentioned in its recap the supposed revolver purchase by writing; "The man and the woman who purchased the revolver are believed to have been J. Morgan Smith and Nan Patterson or J. Morgan Smith and his wife. Evidence was brought out at the first trial of Nan Patterson, to show that Smith had tried to get Nan to do some violence to Young but just what was not clear." All of material was false. Pawnbroker Stern had never identified anyone as the purchaser, having failed twice when he was taken into Nan's presence and an equal number of times when he failed to identify Morgan from a photograph. The last reference was to the newsboy who testified he saw Morgan and Nan together arguing; yet there was nothing else to verify what was a lie on the part of the newsboy or an illusion/delusion.

Still another account noted, with regard to the tailing detective; "Not for a moment after Smith left here [New York City] was he out of sight of the detective, and for a time the sleuth even traveled in Smith's company." Aiken found Smith and his wife in Montreal and became friendly with them; "They knew the nature of his employment but were not aware he was on their trail," said the reporter. Julia Smith talked about the couple's travels; "My husband and I left New York about the middle of last August. We went to Montreal, where Mr. Smith obtained work as an insurance solicitor, In Montreal we stayed in the Welland Hotel. Then we moved to Gravelle's flats where we lived for several months. Mr. Smith was not very successful in the insurance business, and he became a book agent, making trips to Kingston and Belleville, Ontario, I remaining in Montreal." Continuing her store Julia said; "We finally decided to leave Montreal and we went to Toronto. There we met Mr. Aiken. We knew he was a detective by occupation but did not think he had any business with us. From Toronto we went to Hamilton. Mr. Aiken being one of the party. From Hamilton we went to Cleveland by way of Detroit and Toledo. We stayed in the Hollenden House in Cleveland. Mr. Smith went to Nashville and Louisville to see about getting some work with the bookmakers. He was not successful, so we decided to meet in Covington where I have relatives. Mr. Aiken and I came on here [Cincinnati] Wednesday and went to Covington where we meet Mr. Smith in the street. She explained they got no help from those relatives and then returned to Cincinnati and registered at the Grand Hotel; "The arrest was a complete surprise to me."

On the morning of April 1 it was learned that lawyers Thomas

F. Shay and Cogan of Cincinnati who had stepped forward to represent the Smith couple, were retained by Julia's parents, John Patterson and his wife of Washington D. C. The attorneys planned to fight the New York State extradition request. According to the article, which pushed the conspiracy idea, when and if the couple were returned to New York City they would find themselves confronted with affidavits, "made by close friends" that told the story of an alleged conspiracy to extort money from Young, just before his death. The lawyers had advised the Smiths not to talk to anyone about the situation and when Detective Sergeant McNaught, of the New York Police Department, arrived in Cincinnati to question the pair, they would not say a word. A subhead of this article asserted; "close friends tell story of conspiracy to extort money from Young." Nothing was said about whose friends they were and a reader could have inferred they were friends of the Smith but they were all friends of Young and the conspiracy to extort had no evidence behind it, it was all baseless lying.

That same day another breathless account spoke of two "sensational developments" in the case of the Smiths. One was cited as a supposed statement from Mrs. Smith that a fund of $100,000 had been raised for the defence of herself and her husband, although no source for that money was given, or even hinted at. The second was a supposed story that letters in her possession when she was arrested would fall into the hands of District Attorney Jerome and "they may send someone to the chair."

At that point a legal fight began over those letters. Julia was said to have given them over to Aiken for safekeeping around the time the couple were arrested, saying to him; "If these letters get into the hands of the police, they'll hang Nan." According to Aiken, when he received the letters he explained that he supposed they were of minor importance and entirely unconnected with the case and therefore he promised to care for them. Then Mrs. Smith made that remark which caused him to change his mind and he turned the letters over to the local police in Cincinnati, until the material could be delivered to Jerome. Acting for the Smiths, attorney Shay demanded the return of the letters.

Any confidence held by New York State that the Smiths would be quickly extradited from Ohio soon evaporated. On April 2 Assistant District Attorney Garvan said he doubted if the fight to extradite the couple would be concluded soon. "All the complications possible, I believe will be injected into the case by the attorneys for the Smith," he said, "I have no doubt that we shall win out all right but the resistance to us will probably be about to the full limit of the power of the law to overcome it." He added; "Nan Patterson, her family, her friends and her attorneys have as a most important end now the keeping of the Smiths away from New York. The letters Detective Aiken secured from Mrs. Smith are of great importance as evidence." When asked if he had obtained possession of those letters, Garvan would not answer "but smiled knowingly." New York Police Department Detective McNaught, and Garvan, were then both in Cincinnati.

Somewhat ominously a reporter began a piece on the Smiths by declaring; "For some mysterious source there has arisen an influence that has made for J. Morgan Smith and his wife... powerful friends in Cincinnati...When arrested the couple had combined assets on their persons of $3.74. But now they have one of the most prominent firms of criminal lawyers in the city of Cincinnati working on their behalf." According to this account the money sent to Cincinnati was contributed by a prominent Tammany politician; "His interest in the case is said to have been aroused through a woman who knew Nan Patterson and Caesar Young." That woman was supposedly concerned that Nan did not kill Young but she believed that Smith bought the revolver with which the killing was done. Consequently she has determined to bend her efforts to keep Smith away from New York and to that end had obtained the financial support of the Tammany man; "Scores of persons in New York knew of the whereabouts of Smith ever since he disappeared. In nearly every theatrical company that visited Montreal there were persons who knew either Smith or his wife. Smith was soliciting insurance and, he said, making a living." To those who asked Morgan why he had fled he replied that he got a tip that he was to be locked up and held as a witness. Rather than run a chance of spending months in jail awaiting the trial, he decided to flee. However, it was noted that; "To all who spoke to him he denied that he bought the revolver with which the killing was done."

Those by now infamous letters, according to this source, were expected to arrive in New York City in a day or two, having been mailed from Cincinnati. Said Garvan; "The letters that we found in the trunk of Mr. and Mrs. J. Morgan Smith absolutely clinch the case of the State in the Nan Patterson affair." He went on to add; "While no particular letter contains evidence on which conviction could be secured, the entire lot form so strong a chain of evidence as to completely corroborate the case of the prosecution. They positively establish Smith's connection with the alleged plot and really are the most important direct evidence secured in the case as yet. The letters are written by relatives of either Smith or the Pattersons, and while they are worded in guarded language, their meaning is so plain that there is no misunderstanding their purport." When arrested the pair had only $3.74 in cash assets while their bill at the Grand Hotel was $10.50, and thus the luggage of the couple was held in lieu of payment. When attorney Shay learned of the situation he neglected to pay the bill and retrieve the luggage. As soon as Garvan learned of the situation he paid the room bill, got a writ for the trunk, and then came into possession of the letters. In this account no mention was made of Aiken coming into possession of the letters. Said Julia Smith; "I don't care if they have got those letters...my attorney tells me from what I have been able to tell him of their contents that they will have no effect upon the trial of Nan Patterson's case." And, she continued; "I don't care now if I do go back to New York. I will not go voluntarily as a prisoner. I object to that and we will fight to the last...I see that we made a mistake when we ran away.

We should have stayed right there and helped Nan by our testimony."

The package of letters was delivered by the US Postal Service to District Attorney Jerome on April 4. From the size of the package a newsman estimated that it contained perhaps 100 letters. In Cincinnati the habeas corpus proceedings launched by the Smiths continued, with various postponements. New York authorities also swore out a formal warrant against the Smiths charging the couple with being fugitives from justice.

A news account the next day insisted that damaging statements affecting the fate of Nan were contained in the letters received by Assistant District Attorney Rand from Cincinnati. So important were the letters "and so deeply do they incriminate" Nan, it was said, that Rand stated he would go on with the trial of Patterson on the coming Monday [April 10] even if the Smiths could not be brought to New York City in time for the trial. Supposedly reference was made in the letters to the importance of the Smiths remaining in seclusion until after the trial of Nan and "the disastrous effect which would follow if the Smiths were captured and brought to New York." Rand said the nature of the new evidence would not be made public but implied the defense was in for a big surprise.

Another complication in the case developed that day when, stated a journalist; "for some reason known only to the District Attorney's office," Patterson's father was summoned before the Grand Jury. John Patterson was in the Tombs visiting his daughter when he was told that Rand wanted to see him. When he left Rand's office after a meeting that lasted 30 minutes he was served with a subpoena requiring him to appear before the Grand Jury the next day. Another visitor to Rand's office that day was Caesar's widow, Margaret Young. She was in conference with Rand for about an hour. Purpose of that visit was unknown but speculation was that she had an appointment to read some of the letters then in Rand's possession. It was further speculated that some of those letters may have contained revelations about John Patterson. An idea then revived was that there was no reason to believe the father was in ignorance of the whereabouts of his other daughter and his son-in-law "at any time since their disappearance from the city in June last." Also revived was the idea that the father had been responsible for delivering to the Smiths the clothing they needed after they first disappeared and before they started their wandering journey. And it was for that disappearance while under a Grand Jury subpoena that Morgan was indicted for contempt of court. Speculation also arose that an attempt might be made to hold Patterson in contempt, for having aided the Smiths to escape from the jurisdiction of the court. Meanwhile, the Smiths continued to languish in the County Jail in Cincinnati.

On April 6 Jerome still insisted the trial would start on Monday April 10. John Patterson had appeared before the Grand Jury and, noted a reporter; "After the elder Patterson had been examined Mr. Rand could not conceal his jubilation. Nor could the fact that the elder Patterson had revealed secrets under pressure in the Grand Jury room be kept confined with the limits of the District Attorney's office." Daniel O'Reilly, one of Nan's attorneys, said that only two letters from John Randolph Patterson were found in the luggage of Julia Smith when she was arrested. Those letters, he explained, contained no reference to the case of his daughter Nan.

A different account, with respect to John Patterson's testimony before the Grand Jury said; "It is certain, however, that the district attorney hopes to use it to help convict the young woman of murder when she is put on trial next week." When the father appeared before the Grand Jury what was probed, it was believed, was his role in aiding and abetting the flight of the Smiths; "According to the information in the district attorney's office Patterson procured the removal of the baggage of Smith and his wife from the St. Paul Hotel here [New York City] to Meyer's Hotel in Hoboken [New Jersey], and had an interview with the Smiths before they made a rapid flight to Canada." This article then went into several paragraphs of speculation as to what it all meant and what might have happened if Smith had indeed bought the revolver on June 3. Such groundless, baseless speculation amounted to trial by media and worked to undermine any notions that Nan was innocent.

Rand was said to put a good deal of faith in the story that Morgan Smith purportedly told to a newspaper reporter in Montreal that he, Smith, knew pawnbroker Hyman Stern. However, Rand admitted a day or so later, that he was not looking for that reporter to, presumably, verify that story.

In one account about the Smiths, the journalist declared; "J. Morgan Smith, it was disclosed last night, has unwittingly helped to close the net about his sister-in-law..." The newsman reasoned that was where agents of Jerome had scored; "The movements of the Smiths have been traced from the time they left New York until their arrest. Smith, though traveling under an assumed name could not restrain his talkative disposition, and in hotels and other places is said to have discussed the Patterson-Young case freely." Herein it was noted that after John Patterson's appearance before the Grand Jury there were no plans to take any action against the man. While the trial was still supposed to be on schedule to start on April 10 it was true that, as of April 8, no subpoenas had been issued for witnesses. Lawyers Levy and Unger claimed that Nan and her immediate relatives were penniless and for that reason the defense was hampered. Some witnesses would not be called owing to the expense and thus could not be used unless they volunteered their services. Nan's lawyers said they were then working on the case without a fee.

The third trial of Nan Patterson for murder in the first degree was postponed for a week. It had been slated for April 10 but was postponed until Monday April 17. The reason given was that prosecutor Rand was busy with other cases. Meanwhile, on April 10 the Smiths abandoned their fight against extradition and agreed to leave for New York City in the custody of New York Police Department Detective Sergeant McNaught and accompanied by Assistant District Attorney Garvan. They planned to leave Cincinnati for New York on the evening of

April 10. Reportedly, the Smiths agreed to go voluntarily to New York if Garvan would pledge himself that there would be no charges brought against them in the New York courts except that of conspiracy, upon which the indictment that led to their arrest was found. Garvan agreed. That third trial of Nan would be held before Recorder Goff in the Court of General Sessions. Before the postponement was announced a special panel of 200 potential jurors had been summoned but only 143 of the talesmen answered the call and showed up at the court house. By the direction of Recorder Goff, each of the 57 absentees was fined $100.

The Smiths were in the lockup in New York City on the night of Tuesday April 11. Morgan slept in a cell at police headquarters while Julia was sent to the Mercer Street police station, one of the stations that had a matron on duty. The party left Cincinnati on the night of April 10 with the couple placed in the charge of Garvan, McNaught, New York Police Department officer Quinn, and a private detective named Ward. They traveled by train but the pair were taken off the train before it reached Grand Central Station, in anticipation of a crowd that would be there. And it was reported that several hundred people were in fact waiting there to see them, including "a battalion of photographers." By this account there was no agreement made and the Smiths voluntarily returned. Rather, lawyer Thomas F. Shay saw the futility of further extradition battles "and after a consultation with Mr. Garvan at which it was agreed that no effort could be made to extract a confession from them on the journey east. Mr. Shay of their counsel consented to their inevitable return. No agreement or stipulation was made as to their prosecution on any charge other than that contained in the indictment as set forth in the extradition papers." In New York City H. R. Limburger was to represent the Smiths. He said he was asked by John Patterson to represent the couple; "There is not a cent in it for me, as Mr. Patterson told me that he was penniless. I seldom take such cases unless I think it is in a good cause. Now that I have talked with Smith, I can see no reason why he should ever have left town." Added Limburger; "Smith is ready and willing to testify at the trial of Nan Patterson. I think he will help her; I can't see how he can hurt her. There is nothing in the letters taken from the Smiths in Cincinnati that incriminates them or Nan Patterson, from what Smith tells me. I will ask District Attorney Jerome to-morrow to surrender them to me at once." When the pair were booked in New York City Smith said he was an insurance agent aged 30; Julia was 29.

The Smiths were arraigned on conspiracy charges in the Court of General Sessions on April 12 but the case was put off for at least a few days. The pair had bail fixed in the amount of $3,000 each but they would remain in custody as they were not able to furnish bail in any amount. One of those in court when the Smiths were arraigned was pawnbroker Hyman Stern. Before going into the court session that day Stern said he was doubtful if he could identify Morgan or Julia. After he had seen Morgan on this day he said; "What I said before about not being possible goes." That is, he was unable to identify Morgan as the revolver buyer. Nan requested and received permission to see Julia; it was the first meeting of the sisters since the June day of the death of Caesar Young. Both Smiths were lodged in the Tombs. Reportedly, Julia was housed in a cell on the upper tier, where Nan resided, some two doors apart from her younger sister. All three were indicted on the conspiracy charge to extort money from Smith.

The indictment charging Nan, along with the Smiths, to extort money from Young was dismissed on April 14 in the Court of General Sessions, at the respect of Rand. As to the indictment against the Smiths on that charge, the court reserved its decision in that case. Rand explained to the court that a mistake had been made in drawing up the indictment against Nan and that it tended to prejudice her position in the capital case In asking for dismissal of the indictment against Nan, Rand reserved the right to resubmit the indictment. The effect of the action was to prevent her counsel from getting access to the grand jury minutes, which might have aided her defense. Counsel for the Smiths asked the court for an order compelling the District Attorney to return the letters and documents taken from the Smiths. However, the court refused that motion.

In dismissing the conspiracy charge against Patterson (all three were in court together) Rand said to Judge Foster in General Sessions Court; "When the Grand Jury indicted the Smiths they did not want to let Nan Patterson go, as she was equally involved. Yet I feel that another indictment against her might work to her disadvantage in her trial for the murder of Caesar Young, especially if she took the stand in her behalf. She has been in the Tombs for about ten months, which is almost the punishment she would get if she was convicted of conspiracy. Therefore I move to dismiss the indictment." In trying to retrieve the letters attorney Limburger read from one Julia Smith wrote to Young in which she said that Nan was in an "interesting condition." Apparently that was interpreted by the state as "pregnant" and thus that letter formed the basis for the idea of extortion and led to the indictment for conspiracy against the Smiths.

A day before trial number three began a long article appeared that outlined the Smiths' "remarkable flight" from justice. A subhead declared; "Leaving New York last August, they have traveled over half a continent, baffling detectives and eluding pursuit." [Yet not much earlier extensive press coverage was devoted to the story that the Smiths were under surveillance and their whereabouts known for almost all of their disappearance. And, in fact, this article admitted as much]. The article began by stating; "That the Smiths actually eluded pursuit during eight months away from New York can hardly be said with justice to the detective force. They were watched and shadowed by a number of different men during this time. Why the much wanted witnesses in the trial of Nan Patterson were not arrested and brought to New York long ago has, however, not been explained." And; "They returned from Canada where they first sought refuge, many weeks ago and could have been taken into custody at any time. For not only was the detective on their case hot on their trail, but he was traveling with them on the most friendly terms to worm himself into their confidence...There is 'a nigger in the wood pile' somewhere." That is, something was wrong, something was rotten. And, it was observed, in spite of the reports of large sums of money said to be at the disposal of the Smiths, Morgan had to work for his living during his trip to Canada. He spent time working as an insurance salesman and then as a book agent. With a bag of samples he went door to door in Montreal trying to persuade people to invest in the "works of the best authors." The couple used various aliases as they traveled; in Montreal he was Adams, in Detroit he was Collins, in Cleveland he was Robinson, and in Cincinnati he was H. H. Banning.

This account of the events that culminated in the arrest of the couple, given by Morgan Smith, differed from that told by detective Aiken. With respect to Aiken, Morgan said; "We knew who he was and all about him all the time, and what we did we did with our eyes open. The real truth of the matter is that we knew we had to be watched by somebody and we made up our minds that we would rather be watched by Aiken than any of the other detectives that had been trailing us because Aiken seemed the youngest, greenest and easiest to manage...We didn't want to give him the slip. We deliberately informed him in advance of every move we were going to make." Smith claimed it was always the couple's intention to make their way back to New York City and "we fully intended to be there at the proper time for the trial." When they were living in Toronto the pair were shadowed by relays of detectives who were constantly changed and shifted because Julia was good at spotting them as soon as they appeared. On March 17 a new man showed up and Julia spotted him as the latest detective. According to Smith they approached him and told him they knew who he was and what he wanted but they were disposed to be friendly with him and he did not have to worry about sitting up all night watching them because they were perfectly willing to inform him in advance of their movements. The detective was worried his position would be jeopardized if he was seen talking to them but Smith told him he would protect him and the result was that they had dinner together and became friendly. Morgan explained further they they treated him as "a kind of pet" and took him out with them "because he had apparently never been out before and required instruction and enlightenment on the commonest subjects." The Smiths took him out to dinner, and to plays and so forth. Just before the Smiths left Cleveland a detective named Ward appeared on the scene. The article then went on at great length as to what impact Smith would have on the third trial focusing on the letters and the dramatic impact if Stern would be on the stand and point out Smith as the purchaser of the revolver. It was primarily for making Smith face Stern that the authorities wanted Smith in New York City for the trial. That conveniently overlooked the fact that Stern had failed, several times by this point, to identify Smith, both from a photograph and in person. The letters contained no evidence of any kind; they were merely family correspondence saved up over time as many families did.

Mr. and Mrs. (Julia Patterson) J. Morgan Smith, perhaps from police mug shots. They went on to become a very elusive couple.

CHAPTER 7. TRIAL #3.

On April 17 1905 the trial was called but adjourned for 24 hours. It was held before Recorder John W. Goff in the Court of General Sessions. When the trial was called Assistant District Attorney Gans asked for a delay stating that; "matters of a delicate nature had arisen which would make it impossible for the people to commence the case today."When Goff commented that the state's reasons for an adjournment seemed "very vague," Gans replied that a most extraordinary action had been brought in another county which he said had made it necessary for the district attorney to ask for an adjournment. That other issue was thought to be about the letters as a restraining order had been issued to compel the District Attorney to hand over the letters to their owners.

Coinciding with the supposed first day of trial number three was a article about the background of Ann Elizabeth Patterson. It was fairly long and reinforced some facts from previous sketches of the woman, presented some new facts; and, contradicted some of the earlier material published about her. The piece began by describing her as a bareheaded young girl running wild in the fields and forests of a Virginia plantation. As a child she loved the solitude of the woods and the hills and slopes of rural retreats; "She was always out of doors with sunbonnet strung around her throat and dangling on her back. Her face was bronzed by the sun, and she was known throughout the countryside as a romping, rustic sprite." Born in Washington D. C., less than 23 years earlier, while she was a child her father took the family to the county beyond the Potomac to live. Nan grew up on a farm and reveled in rural life as any city born girl would at that age. She was described as always athletic and having never tired of her romps through the woods. Those who knew Nan as the bareheaded wood sprite of Virginia and even those who knew her as a schoolgirl in Washington a few years later "marvel as they ponder on the transformation that evolved the 'Nan Patterson of the Floradora sextet" and the 'Nan Patterson, prisoner at the bar.'" According to this account the Pattersons were "prominent. Her uncle was a United States Senator – the late J. W. Patterson of New Hampshire who served from 1867 to 1873. Her father, John Randolph Patterson, held many public offices in Washington and at the time Nan left the farm to return to the city for education John was chief clerk to the supervising architect of the United States. The Pattersons were related to another "prominent family", the Randolphs of Virginia.

Reportedly, Nan had little trouble mastering her lessons as a schoolgirl "but the life she had led in the country left little fondness for books in her mind, and she gave nearly all of her time to athletic and outdoor sports, paying only sufficient attention to her studies to grasp the general benefits of each lesson and make her records good before the class." Around this time she became "stage struck...She wanted to go out in the world and make a name, win the plaudits of the world, triumph as an artist..." To further upset her and and misdirect her life came her first love affair at his time and Nan "was helpless in deciding on any sensible purpose in life...she listened to every word her first sweetheart poured into her willing ears about the future of their two lives, and the two lovers, after building castles in the air during a brief courtship, ran away and were married." At 17 [actually 16] Nan married Leon Martin. He was from Syracuse and worked for a railroad at the time. Left unsaid was the fact that Martin was about 14 years older than her; he was 30 or 31. As a result of the marriage she was temporarily estranged from her home and family as the family never reconciled to the marriage. That marriage was unhappy from the start and her old longing for the stage came back as the marriage soured. She managed to have a few minor stage appearances but when she was engaged to sing in the sextet of the second *Floradora* company she "was practically unknown to stage folk." However, she "had at that time been on the stage sufficiently long to have caught the craving for a life of luxury, of Bohemian revelry during the small hours of morning, of finery, carriage drives, champagne suppers and all those things which are the essentials of the 'pace that kills.'" When she went on the road as an actor she met Frank Thomas Young and a flirtation started as soon as they met. She yielded so completely to that infatuation "that she lost even that ambition to win fame which had misdirected her life at the age of sixteen." Herein it says that Nan knew from the moment she met him that he was married. It also stated that Young was as infatuated with Nan as she was with him.

And so, on Tuesday April 18 1905, Nan Patterson was called to the bar for once again, to be tried for murder in the first degree, for the third time. Her father John was present as he had been for every day that she had been in court. However, this time he was told to sit in the body of the courtroom with the spectators, behind the counsel table. Up to that time John had always been allowed to sit at the defendant's table, with his daughter and her lawyers. In describing her appearance during this call to the bar one reporter exclaimed; "Nan Patterson has changed. Prison life has agreed with her. Even the court officers started when they saw the actress, now grown stout almost to the point of pudginess." Talesmen were asked the same questions on the same topics as at all the previous trials: such as being questioned as to the weight they give to circumstantial evidence; if the fact that the defendant was a woman would influence their judgment; and did they have any qualms about imposing the death penalty on a woman. Potential jurors were also questioned closely as to the state of their health, apparently the outcome of trial number one still haunted them. Defense lawyers always asked a talesman if it were shown that the defendant had led an immoral life, would that fact prejudice them against the prisoner.

Another description of the prisoner remarked; "At the opening of the day's proceedings the young actress stepped to the bar with elastic step, shining eyes and smiling mouth. She is plumper even than when she appeared at the last time in December." The headline of the piece said; "Nan Patterson wants jury of married men," although the text of the article said nothing whatsoever about the topic. This account also mentioned that a burglar who was sentenced just before her case started said to her, as he passed by, "Hope you win, Miss." Thomas Nolan was the burglar in question and he was brought to the bar while his verdict was read out. However, Nan was not then in court as her trial did not start until the Nolan case was disposed of. During that period Nan was held in another area of the courthouse and she and Nolan never met, or passed each in the hall or corridor.

A reporter by the name of Marlen E. Pew delivered an opinion piece about the prisoner, at the start of the trial. Pew declared the expert criminologist who read human character from the lines and mold of the face and head and hands found in Nan "very little evidence of a weakness or moral blunt" and she "would be the last person in the crowd whom one would naturally point out as the central figure in such a tragedy" as the death of Young. And, the piece continued, she was the same Nan as when taken into custody nearly a year ago; "Her appearance and manner suggest the typical Broadway show girl on parade, well kept, well fed, frivolous and gay, rather than a fear-struck, hysterical supplicant for life and freedom." Pew added; "The nearest she comes to showing fearful emotion is when, attacked by the harsh tongue of the prosecuting attorney, she shapes her pretty face into a sort of timorous pout or cringes with a jerky impulsiveness toward her gray haired father who sits by her side. Once in a while she weeps softly." Concluded Pew; "The girl does not appear mentally strong enough or possessed of sufficient cunning to perpetuate the crime charged against her, or, if so, to bind it in such a web of mystery."

The old canard about Patterson selecting the jury was raised yet again for the third time in her third trial. According to the account; "Miss Patterson personally directs examination and rejection of talesmen," and "The former actress personally directed the selection of the jurors by the defense." An account in a different newspaper also emphasized that false story. One of its subheads declared that Nan; "Tells her counsel jurors who will decide her fate must be to her liking."

Emmeline Pendennis was a journalist who drew the following conclusion after a talk with Patterson; "Is Nan Patterson the murderer of Caesar Young? If so, she does not look the part. The loud, bold unlovely woman I had expected to see was effaced from my mind, and in place of the false conception stood the real Nan or the new Nan, a sweet-faced girl, repentant or victimized by injustice, humiliated but hopeful of release."

Late in the day on April 19 the jury selection was completed and once again Nan would face a jury almost entirely composed of married men, only two of the 12 were single, one a bachelor and one a widower. Most of the jury members were middle age or beyond Many of them had large families, some with daughters who were married; "Her counsel declares that the girl is well pleased with the jury. Throughout the day she had evinced the keenest interest in the examination of the talesmen." Showing an interest is not the same, of course, as selecting.

In total 94 talesmen were examined before the process was completed, compared with almost 200 men for trial number two. Forty-two of the 60 peremptory challenges allowed to both sides were used (30 allowed each side) with the defense using 24 of its peremptory challenges while the prosecution used 18 of its challenges. The remainder were all dismissed for cause. This account observed that expected prosecution witnesses John Millin and Margaret Young "will not be let off as easily this time as at the last trial. Mrs. Young was not cross-examined at all when she was on the witness stand before but this time Mr. Levy will put her through severe questioning."

Arguing the case for the prosecution in trial number three were Assistant District Attorneys William H. Rand Jr., and Francis P. Garvan. On the side of Nan Patterson were Abraham Levy, Henry W. Unger, Daniel O'Reilly, Philip Waldheimer, and the heretofore not mentioned George Simpson. The presiding Judge was Recorder John W. Goff. And, almost unbelievably, yet another "eye-witness" who saw Young fire that shot that killed him, emerged from the darkness. Court was not in session over the long Easter weekend and perhaps that slow news period with respect to the trial helped to explain, this time, the silliness that would not die. This tale came out of Chicago on April 21. B. Rosen of Chicago wrote the New York Police Department to say that he knew a man who saw the shooting. He was referring to his brother-in-law Samuel Eisenberg, who came to Chicago two weeks earlier. The latter could not speak English and his story was given to a reporter through an interpreter. Eisenberg claimed to have seen the whole thing, the struggle and then Young shooting himself. Then he got scared and ran away. He remained in New York City, however, until two weeks earlier. While there in New York he worked for the Pennsylvania Railroad. After he reached Chicago he happened to read, in a Yiddish newspaper, about the Patterson case coming up for trial number three. He was sure it was what he saw and told his brother-in-law Rosen about it. Rosen then wrote to the police. Eisenberg was described as about 37 years old and was of the laboring class of Russian Jews. He came to the United States from Russia a little over a year ago, landing at New York City and had been there for about three months when the shooting took place. He said he remained silent because he knew nothing about American justice and worried he would end up in jail if he told his story. Pointedly, this piece sagely noted that Eisenberg's story tallied exactly with that of the tale from "witness" Hazelton."

One day later the silly season was extended when the same newspaper that "broke" the Eisenberg tale gave another account of Eisenberg's supposed witnessing. This time a three-panel illustration in the newspaper showed the struggle with real people standing in for Nan and Caesar. Reportedly, counsel for Nan was to send a representative to Chicago to interview Samuel Eisenberg and if it made sense they would bring him to New York to testify. Moving on to a lie of a different color this same piece declared that Patterson had suddenly got religion. According to this part of the tale; "Those who have witnessed Nan Patterson's every move declare that her religion is not a pose, and base their statements on the fact that the girl prays constantly in secret." Perhaps a contradiction lay in that last sentence. Abraham Levy did not dispatch one of his people to Chicago, rather he contacted a Chicago lawyer who went to see Eisenberg. And there the matter ended because Levy's only comment after the Chicago man had spoken to Eisenberg was that the latter was "unsatisfactory.

More hit pieces and articles that smeared Patterson began to appear. One of them came from the pen of journalist Emmeline Pendennis who described the prisoner as follows; "no one who had spoken to her, or even seen her, would for a moment hesitate to describe her as far from intellectual – even unintelligent or dull...But in Nan's past she seems to have thought little, even felt little. She is one of those pleasure-loving, happy-go-lucky people – the world's grown up children – who face no problems, fight no battles, obey no law but that of their own light hearts." Pendennis continued by writing; "Yes, Nan has lost her old-time chorus-girl air, much of her vivacity, but has gained instead a modesty and sweetness of demeanor that are infinitely more appealing" Then Pendennis modified that supposed compliment by asserting; "The strain of the situation and the consciousness of the penetrating gaze of the cruel – men searching her for some answering clue to the unanswered question, 'Did you kill Caesar Young or not?' as she sits beside her counsel so quietly and calm, one realizes that her composed features form a mask for none too calm a mood." After pointing out that Nan's lack of exercise and the close confinement had robbed her of rosy cheeks and that she was growing much too fat Emmeline concluded; "On the whole, Nan Patterson is the sort of young woman who seems quite out of place in a criminal court. Her personality is naturally so light, so care-free so careless that it strikes one as absurd that she should be held accountable for what might have been crime, accident or, as she affirms, suicide, whether guilty or not."

One day later Emmeline had another piece published about the defendant. She began by saying; "It seems to me that about the strongest testimony in Nan's defense is her own mental and emotional make-up. There are certain psychological reasons why Nan Patterson is not only incapable of conceiving the murder of Caesar Young, but of carrying so foul a plot into execution." As far as Pendennis was concerned Nan could not attain such intensity of feeling needing for the killing. She did not have the nerve and impetuosity. While Emmeline admitted Nan was jealous it was not strong enough to motivate a murder on June 4 because she cared for Young as much as she ever had. Her life was comprised of "superficial emotions" only and not deep enough to inspire a murder. Agreeing that Nan had been called a "bad" woman, Pendennis thought there was nothing vicious about her; "She is one of those pathetic but lovable figures that are unfit to shape their own destinies and quite dependent upon their environment, that forms them as it will. Never has she been bad; she has been indiscreet, lax and careless, but all through a perfectly comprehensible series of events." Rather, Emmeline labeled her a "spoiled child" who was allowed to have more of her own way than was good for her. The whole affair, Pendennis concluded; "was a great disaster, and it has cast a dark spell over Nan's life that will not easily be lifted. But who shall say Nan brought it on herself."

The trial proper got underway on Monday April 24 when Rand presented the state's case. For the third time within six months the young woman sat in court and heard the story of her life being outlined to a jury, and of all the events leading up to the death of Caesar. Reportedly, Nan "flinched before the burning words. It was a bitter ordeal, and there was no father at her side to aid her in the tense moments. By the court's order the old man has been forced to sit without the rail." As in the past trials the courtroom was crowded to the doors with long lines of people steaming into the building. Some favored few, with friends at court, were permitted to enter, but scores were turned away. Rand said, in his opening remarks, that her "loose morals" should not be held against her but that, of course, the character of her life had to be considered as bearing upon the case and the weight of evidence. Rand added that he would show the murder of Young was planned the day before the shooting. The prosecutor spoke of Julia and of her marriage to J. Morgan Smith. Morgan, he said, came from a good family but since the man had graduated from college, he had gone "steadily downhill." Rand explained to the jury that there was a conspiracy by which it was intended to have Young continue to support the defendant and to keep him from his wife. Said the prosecutor; "Smith is the chief actor in this tragedy next to Nan Patterson.

Also on April 24, Supreme Court Justice Gaynor handed down a decision denying the motion of the Smiths for the return of the letters seized in Cincinnati. Initially he had ordered the letters returned but Jerome protested and was given an opportunity to show cause why the letters should not be returned. After hearing those arguments, Gaynor reversed his decision saying it had not been shown that the Smiths needed the letters then in the hands of Jerome, in order to properly prepare their defense, and therefore the motion was denied. The Smiths continued to be represented by Herbert R. Limburger. The Smiths had been married early in 1903.

Another over-the-top exaggeration about Nan and her reaction in court supposed came on April 24 when the defendant was supposedly overcome by Rand's declaration that her brother-in-law, Morgan Smith, bought the revolver with which Young was shot; "Nan Patterson collapsed on reaching her cell in the Tombs this afternoon and fell fainting into the arms of her sister." Before she left the courtroom at the end of the morning session she appeared faint and "as she had difficulty in breathing, the windows were thrown open." Even that did not revive her and her counsel pleaded for an early adjournment, which was granted.

In another account it was observed that Nan seemed ready to faint at the close of Rand's opening statement at which time Goff order a recess. The windows of the courtroom were opened to admit more air; "The prisoner appeared to be as well as usual when the talking of testimony was begun in the afternoon." That discomfort came after Rand made the "significant declaration" that the revolver that killed Young was bought by Morgan on June 3. And that the killing of Young was the result of a plot to keep the bookmaker from leaving the country. Young had been supporting the Smiths as well as Nan, Rand asserted.

Another account about Rand and his opening remarks was that his outline for trial number three "was practically a repetition of those which had gone before it..." Feeling faint at the end of Rand's remarks she called her lawyers Levy and Unger and gasped; "I am ill and I am afraid I shall faint if I am not allowed to rest." Levy informed Goff and a recess was ordered. When the trial resumed in the afternoon, however, "she appeared to have fully recovered from the attack." Rand's opening remarks were virtually the same as in trials number one and number two except for the increasing use of the Smiths, over time, as they drew more and more of Rand's attention as major players in Young's death. Rand even went so far as to argue that during the year Caesar maintained Nan he spent $50,000 on his mistress.

Another example of trial by media could be seen in an article that appeared on April 25. It was titled; "Attorney Rand welding chain about actress." A subhead to the piece asserted; "Sledgehammer blows of prosecutor cause Nan Patterson to abandon the calm demeanor previously displayed." But there was nothing new presented in the case; it was the same old case in the same old way, except for the references to "the letters" and the attention paid to the Smiths. The letters contained nothing whatsoever and were hardly used in the trial. The material on the Smiths was completely manufactured and no evidence ever existed for the attack by the prosecution on the Smiths. That all died in court as well.

During this trial, for the second time, "experts" used a skeleton in court to show the path of the bullet, although it had much less impact on Patterson; "The skeleton had less effect on her than on the two score women spectators. The women were lined around the back of the court room...The production of the skeleton evidently furnished one of the sensations they had been hoping for."

Hyman Stern, the pawnbroker, was called to the stand on April 26 and failed to identify Morgan Smith as the man who bought the revolver with which Young was killed. Confrontation between the pair had been looked to with great anticipation, as likely to be sensational "but instead it was tame and commonplace." When Stern was on the stand both Smiths were brought before him but he could not identify either as part of the couple who had bought the weapon. And, of course, Stern had failed to identify the Smiths on earlier occasions, several times. He had also failed to identify Nan more than once and he also failed to identify Young, from a photo.

In a piece that analyzed the Stern appearance at the trial a reporter noted that the appearance was expected to be the prosecution's trump card. It had been widely held that the presence in court of Smith would convict the girl of murder. When Smith fled before the first trial the state bewailed his absence and declared that only his presence was necessary to permit them to put into evidence that which, without doubt, would result in a conviction. Failure by the jury to reach an agreement, such people professed to believe, was almost entirely due to the fact that Smith had not been found. Said the journalist; "Through all the months a ceaseless search for the missing witness was prosecuted and finally, just before the girl was going to face her accusers, Smith and his wife were tracked to Cincinnati, arrested as fugitives from justice..." It was reported here that nearly $30,000 was spent by the District Attorney's office in the search for the Smiths.

The Stern testimony fizzled out immediately but anticipation of fireworks ensured a large crowd. Wrote a journalist; "There was a greater crowd than ever at the trial yesterday.

Women fought with men to get into the courtroom. A juror who couldn't fight his way in at the afternoon session was so incensed that he complained to Recorder Goff." And that was about all that happened. However a different newspaper produced its usual highly exaggerated account of the same event Herein the title of the piece was; "Nan Patterson court in riot." According to the text; "There was an actual riot in the Criminal Courts Building at the Nan Patterson trial this afternoon which continued for nearly an hour...Women screamed and some fainted. Men kicked and punched, and even when policemen threatened arrest kept on fighting...Three jurors begged for elbow room and were punched in the stomach in return."

When Margaret Young took the stand she testified that she first learned of the relationship between Nan and her husband Caesar Young in January 1903. Apparently, the defense didn't bother to cross-examine this witness to any extent.

At 3:00 PM on April 28 the prosecution closed its case. After a conference by Patterson's lawyers it was decided, and then announced, that no defense would be put in. The defendant stood ready to submit her case to the jury." According to one account the most sensational and dramatic scene took place when Julia Smith; "with a ring of defiance in her voice, declared that she would remain loyal to her sister and rejected Mr. Rand's offer to have the conspiracy indictment against her dismissed at once if she freely would answer his questions." Those infamous letters seized in Cincinnati and which supposedly proved the Smiths were involved in the purchase of the gun involved in the death of Caesar were introduced by Rand but Recorder Goff refused to admit them as evidence.

None of Rand's attempts at presenting overwhelmingly evidence against Nan had worked or even come close. One of his motifs, in earlier trials, was that Nan was "a woman scorned," yet nothing in the way of evidence backed up such a claim. His latter reliance on dragging the Smiths into the case failed dismally. As in the above paragraph he was reduced to confronting Julia Smith not with evidence but with an attempt at bribery

– tell me what I want to hear and I will quash that conspiracy indictment, which, of course, gives some idea of why that indictment was created in the first place. Pawnbroker Stern had about 10 attempts (with live people and/or photographs) with at least four different people but could not identify anybody at anytime. Rand knew that but, nonetheless, built his case for trial number three mostly on that speculation. After Rand rested his case and before the defense announced there would be no defense mounted Patterson's counsel moved the case be dismissed as Rand had not proved his assertions. However, Rand argued against that motion, stating; "I don't believe that there is a person within the hearing of my voice who doubts that J. Morgan Smith bought that pistol and I am far from yielding that branch of the case." The entire Stern aspect brought up the question of whether Stern really sold the death revolver on June 3. Supposedly that had been proven because the pawnbroker had entered in his records the serial number of the revolver in question. That number was supposedly entered accurately in his accounts as having been sold on June 3. Almost certainly he did not sell the revolver. Did Stern come across the serial number perhaps in some news article about the killing and, for unknown reasons, enter it in his own books? It certainly generated much publicity for Stern and his business. Or was that number given surreptitiously to Stern by the police or some other official in the know? None of the principals in the case had much of an opportunity to buy a revolver on June 3. Cartridges in Young's truck, verified by a reliable source, indicated he owned a 32-caliber weapon and probably had done so for some time.

Monday May 1 marked the final day of the trial with only the summations left to deliver. Nan's counsel was so confident of victory that they offered no defense at all, was the opinion of one observer, unlike at trial number two when Nan took the stand herself. They were content to stand or fall of what evidence the state had produced. Levy went first in the summation process and said, with regard to Rand; "What I have to fear is that you will be fascinated by the blandishments of my opponent who may seek to blind you to the evidence...He should have been fair with this defenseless girl and he should have been fair to you, who lean on him for guidance and not misguidance." He mentioned that the prosecutor Rand had said, before the trial, that he would prove that Young had spent $50,000 on Nan during their time together. Yet no such evidence was introduced.

In his summation lawyer Abraham Levy spoke for five hours and a different reporter noted that; "He attempted no flights of oratory and made few efforts to excite sympathy for his client in the minds of the jury, but from the beginning to the end his address consisted of cold reasoning from the testimony presented by the prosecution that the evidence failed to show the murder of Caesar Young in the first place, and that there was no reason to believe Young shot himself by accident, while he might have shot himself by design." Levy also scored Rand for trying to make the jury believe that Smith pawned some jewelry belonging to his wife on June 3, at the time the pistol was supposedly sold. However, the pawn tickets in evidence showed the jewelry was pawned in October of 1903, long before the alleged revolver purchase.

Journalist Marlen E. Pew offered his thoughts on the case after it was over but before it went to the jury. Pew was a well-known and respected journalist of the era. He said; "Without attempting to forecast so doubtful a quantity as the verdict of a jury in such a complicated case as that of Nan Patterson it may be said with conservatism that there is barely a possibility that she will be convicted upon the state's present evidence." As far as Pew was concerned the best points in her favor were handed out by Rand himself. For one thing his great trump card fell flat when Stern failed to identify Smith. The coroner found powder marks on Young's right hand but failed to discover powder marks on Nan, or to smell its fumes on here. Before the case was half in, Pew canvassed 18 New York newspaper reporters who had heard and weighed every word of evidence and they concluded; "that the case against Nan Patterson had collapsed."

And he added; "it is just the plain fact that Nan Patterson is a shallow-minded girl, without the capacity of comprehending the real and possible peril of her position." Pew also argued that; "Nan gets her cue for the expression of slight emotion from the morbid curiosity seekers who pack the courtroom at every session...It is time for Nan to jerk her face in defiance when the mawkish sentimentalists buzz; time for her to pout or sniffle a little when a dropped pin can be heard." Mentioning the crowds Pew noted that hundreds of men and women daily crowded the street under the pedestrian overpass to catch a glimpse of Nan as she passed over the "Bridge of Sighs." And; "Another pack of scandal wolves clamor at the doors of the courtroom, morning and noon...in a bestial rush for admittance." The scene of stern justice, he argued; "is turned into a bedlam, twice a day by one of the most disgraceful exhibitions of inflamed morbidity a New York court has ever seen...The impressive dignity of the court is made a theater frolic." As well, Pew described the "pathetic figure" of the father, always in the background sitting in the gallery. A patient man there all day, every day, "blind to any faults of his daughter, never critical," and so on. Pew believed he had been disallowed from sitting beside Nan for this trial because the state worried he might create sympathy for Nan, "this old man with his overwhelming love for his daughter – and thus he was banished from the front bench." He argued that the banishment might have been a mistake because the jury was still aware of his presence.

Recorder Goff delivered his charge to the jury of May 3. He told the members of the jury they should not consider the past life of the defendant and that the question was whether or not the defendant killed Young. The jury was not to speculate whether or not Young shot himself. At 1:00 PM that day the jury filed out to begin deliberations. At 2:08 PM the panel went for lunch and left the restaurant at 3:30 PM with what was reported as a "big crowd" following them back to the criminal courts building. At 4:30 PM the jury was still out with rumors then that the jury stood at eight to four for acquittal.

According to a different account the jury had lunch at Hann's Restaurant and the size of the crowd that followed them up the street was 3,000. At 8:00 PM the jury filed out again for a meal, once again going to Hann's Restaurant. This account repeated the speculation that the vote at lunchtime had stood at eight to four for acquittal but the same article remarked that at 11:00 PM the jury stood at seven to five for conviction.

On Thursday May 4 at 2:30 AM the jury reported to Goff that they were unable to agree and the Recorder discharged them. From 10:05 PM the evening before when the jury returned from their meal, until 12:30 AM not a word was heard from the jury. At 1:20 AM the jury filed into the courtroom. Nan was sent for and soon arrived in the courtroom. When she appeared the jury told Goff they could not agree. Goff sent them back to try again. However, no agreement could be reached and about an hour later Recorder Goff dismissed them and trial number three ended the same way as did trial number one and trial number two – with a mistrial. No official vote tally was released but rumor had it that the majority of the jurors had voted for acquittal.

Perhaps some early use of photograph manipulation techniques, imposing Nan's head onto a sketch

CHAPTER 8. AFTER TRIAL # 3, BEFORE FREEDOM.

It was understood, after trial number three, that Nan would at once be released on bail and would not again be brought to trial. That the indictment against her would be quashed. At least it was understood by the journalist who wrote this piece. The idea was that Patterson would be released either on a nominal bail or on her own recognizance, or at least that was what this reporter believed the state inferred when asked earlier in the trial what would happen in the jury hung in this third trial.

Even at this late date new "witnesses" kept popping up. From Sacramento California came a report of a resident of that city who would not give his name to the press but claimed he knew personally that Caesar Young was the owner of a pistol, that he frequently saw the weapon, and even once borrowed it to go hunting. He said he would be available to be subpoenaed in the event yet another trail was held.

One account published the speculation that the last ballot by the jury had been 11 for conviction (manslaughter) and one vote for acquittal. That caused a reporter to remark; "Though the jury stood so overwhelmingly for conviction, which would mean a retrial in any case, the public sentiment and sympathy would swing so strongly to the girl, three times brought to trial, that the purpose of justice itself would be defeated were she called to the bar again...a retrial would partake of persecution, not prosecution. This account then presented more speculation about the vote tallies having it that after about 25 ballots had been taken the jury stood at seven for manslaughter in the first degree and five for acquittal. It was even said that for several hours the vote had been even at six to six, and then one vote shifted over to guilty of manslaughter.

A couple of days after the jury was dismissed it was reported that Nan had received "a dozen offers" to bail her out – altogether she had received 21 letters from people who volunteered to come to her assistance in one form or another. During the day her lawyers received "a score of other offers" to post her bond, in sums ranging from $5,000 to $20,000. Lawyers Levy and O'Reilly spent some of the day on May 5 searching for Rand and/or Garvan to try and arrange Nan's release, but could not find either one of the Assistant District Attorneys – both were reported as out of the office "resting." Also on May 5, Judge Foster dismissed the indictment for conspiracy against the Smiths. J. Morgan Smith remained under indictment on charges of contempt of court in disobeying a Grand Jury subpoena and fleeing New York City the previous June. The penalty on that charge was 30 days' imprisonment, a $100 fine, or both. In this account Levy was cited as saying the jury vote stood at eight to four for acquittal. When Foster dismissed the indictment of conspiracy against the Smiths that judge declared there was no evidence to base the charge on and that it was evidently trumped up for the purpose of extraditing the Smiths from Cincinnati. Said Foster; "The minutes of testimony herein before the Grand Jury disclose no evidence whatsoever of conspiracy on the part of the defendants. The Grand Jury had no right to find an indictment when there was no evidence to support it. I can only explain the fact that an indictment was found on the theory that because the defendants were without the State, and were needed as witnesses in an important case the Grand Jury forgot both the law and their judicial position, and feeling that the end justified the means indicted the defendants that they might be brought here by extradition." In his application for dismissal lawyer Herbert Limburger, for the Smiths, said he understood Rand, at the time, had told the Grand Jury he could convict Nan if he could get the Smiths to New York City and that he wanted the indictment for that purpose. There was also a rumor afoot about the District Attorney's office that Comptroller Grout had complained of the "awful" expense of Jerome's assistants and detectives at Cincinnati, in effecting the arrest of the Smiths.

Another one of Nan's sisters, Mrs. Harriet T. Lowell of Washington D. C., had kept a low profile during the case and had not drawn any attention from the press. At this time, early in May, it was reported that she had been raising funds to provide for the defense of her sister.

On May 6 Patterson had just one visitor. That caller was Eva Booth, commander of the Salvation Army in America. Many people called at the Tombs wanting to see Nan, mostly "cranks," but all were denied admission. That visit marked the first time Booth had ever met the prisoner. She told a reporter; "I am sure that Nan Patterson is not a murderess. She is a finer fiber than one who would commit a wanton crime. Coroner's physician Dr. O'Hanlon, who testified for the prosecution and gave as his opinion that Young could not have killed himself modified that statement in conversation with friends, declaring; "Now that the trial is over I feel free to say that it is my opinion and has been all along that Young had the pistol in his hand when he was shot." An unidentified letter from one of the jury members was left at the court building addressed to William T. Jerome, District Attorney, and reportedly rebuked him and his assistant for going away over the few days after jury dismissal and thus being unavailable to consult with Nan's counsel in order to start the process of releasing the detainee. Herein, in that juror's letter it was stated that the final vote by the jury was eight to four for acquittal.

A bit more of the background of the Nan and Caesar relationship was released at this time. Nan came east, from California, in March 1904 and went to live with her sister Julia Smith. Then she went to Los Angeles where she reunited with her lover, after he sent her a telegram to return west. They parted after he arranged to meet her at the Wellington Hotel in Chicago. When they met there they continued east together and separated at Harrisburg Pennsylvania with Nan going on alone to Washington and Young proceeding on his own to New York City. Nan remained in Washington until May 2 and then came to New York City with her sister Julia. They went to live at the Hotel Navarre and Young called on Nan a few days after her arrival there. Nan had been there only a short time when Young's brother-in-law McKean called on her and said that Margaret Young wanted her to part from Caesar. McKean wanted to send her to Europe and she agreed to make the trip under the belief that Young also desired that outcome.

Abraham Levy held a conference with William Rand on the morning of May 8 in order to have the accused released on either a nominal bail or on her own recognizance. Rand told Levy that he would not be able to make a definite statement about the intention of the prosecution until he talked with District Attorney Jerome, who would be in the city that afternoon. Meanwhile, at about the same time, lawyer Limburger appeared before Justice Foster and submitted a motion for the release of the Smiths. However, at the same time Assistant District Attorney Perkins submitted a motion that the Smiths be held until it could be determined whether the District Attorney desired to re-indict them. Foster, of the Court of General Sessions, took both motions under advisement.

The next day District Attorney William Jerome issued a statement; "I am willing to make any statement other than this: My information in regard to the case presents a serious question for my decision and one which I must decide myself and not permit the newspapers to decide for me. I have not yet decided." In response Levy said; "We have been assured by Mr. Jerome that he will give the matter his earliest consideration. Pending this time there will be no steps taken by us to release Nan on bail. I have a bondsman ready..."

One week after the jury disagreed in the Patterson case a reporter visited her in her cell at the Tombs where she remained. That reporter remarked; "To a reporter Miss Patterson, in the Tombs today, seemed to enjoy the permission given by her counsel to discuss her own case if she felt so inclined." Of course, that was something of a tacit admission that all the supposed conversations published over the course of her incarceration in which much of her "conversations" with journalists were published in quotation marks, were almost all simply lies and manufactured dialog. On this day Patterson said to the reporter; "Mr. Rand seems so bitterly my enemy. He seems to feel so certain that I have been and am the most vicious of women." She added; "I am an innocent woman, and so I cannot understand why the juries at both of my trials were not able to decide that way and let me go...Mr. Rand made such a great effort – twisting every little unhappy circumstance in my unhappy life into such shape – that it seems some of them believe I killed Caesar Young."

Then suddenly it all ended. On Friday May 12 Ann Elizabeth Patterson was released from the Tombs on her own recognizance. At the same time the Smiths were also both released from custody. Shortly after 11:00 AM that day Jerome had Nan brought before Recorder Goff and made a motion that she be allowed to go free on her own recognizance. That motion was granted. In making the motion Jerome stated; "I feel that my assistants have done their duty by the people. I have read all the evidence and it has my full approval – I would have presented the case in the same way. Mr. Rand did right and acted efficiently." He went on to state that he had information; "which permits of no doubt that there was a uniformity of opinion in the jury's mind on three points": the first point being that Morgan Smith bought the revolver; the second point being that Nan took the revolver into the cab with her; and the third point was that Young did not commit suicide. Jerome continued; "In the face of all that an honorable gentleman has been criticized for doing his duty." He added that he did not believe any other outcome would happen in any subsequent trial. Jerome attacked the criticism leveled at Rand and said the trial did not cost anything like $100,000 as reported. Said Goff to Nan; "The motion is made in accordance with the best interest of justice, but in granting the motion I do not want you to take it as an acquittal. I shall make no expression of your weaknesses, and I think that the ordeals that you have undergone in two trials must have been severe." He added; "I hope when you look back on these experiences you will be constrained to lead a life of chastity. You are discharged." An hour of so later in a different courtroom, before Judge Foster, the Smiths saw the conspiracy charges against them finally quashed and the pair were discharged. Foster also ordered the immediate re-arrest of J. Morgan Smith on the contempt of court charge.

Upon the re-arrest of Morgan Smith he was returned to the Tombs. While there he reconsidered his situation and decided to plead guilty to the contempt charge. He was taken back to court that same day and when he appeared before Judge Cowling he was fined $250. A little later that afternoon his fine was paid and he was released from custody.

An editorial on the release of Patterson, published on the day she regained her freedom had this to say; "The release of Nan Patterson is a relief to the public. The state had two opportunities to establish its case against her, and it failed. Her release is the only decent action to take, under the circumstances."

John Randolph Patterson embraces and consoles his daughter on the occasion of the third mistrial in a row for his daughter

CHAPTER 9.
AFTERMATH.

When Nan was released she went to her old address, the St. Paul Hotel, at 60th Street and Columbus Avenue. From there she was expected to soon go on to Washington D. C. According to this account the hotel was surrounded by thousands of people who had turned out to see her. Reportedly the people in the crowd broke into applause. In what was perhaps an understatement, District Attorney Jerome came forward to insist the trial number three, to that point, had cost the state $8,000.

In a different story of her first hours of freedom it was said that she left the Tombs in a cab immediately for the office of her main counsel, Levy and Unger, and found herself "heartily cheered by more than two thousand people." Then, after visiting the offices of Levy and Unger, Nan, her sister Julia, and her father John, went to the St. Paul Hotel where they met some old friends and then they all went shopping. During that first evening Nan stayed in the hotel with her family until around 10:00 PM when the four of them (Morgan Smith had joined them by then) left the hotel and went to a restaurant. After a meal the party arrived at the train station at 12:25 AM the next day and the entire party boarded a train and started off for Washington D. C. Reportedly; "About a hundred persons gathered to see them off."

The party arrived at the Washington train station at 7:20 AM where the group found a crowd of about 1,000 people were waiting to meet them. Said Nan; "I have said frequently that I would never go back to the stage. I am now so beset by offers, however, that I think I will have to yield. I am drawn one way to the footlights, and in another way I have been drawn from them." She added; "On the one hand my father is old and he is poor; he has barely enough to keep him and my dear old mother comfortable. On the other hand I am offered large sums of money to go upon the stage. As I look at it now, money may make the last days of my parents happy and contented." According to Patterson; "I had hardly been out of prison before I received from theatrical managers a dozen offers to go out upon a vaudeville circuit. Though I have never been anything but a chorus girl, they offered me more than a prima donna's salary. Many said, as if they sincerely meant it, that they could put me on the stage and make me famous as an actress. I know, however, that my fame is merely in my notoriety...Since my arrest I have incurred great obligations. I owe to my counsel, to my family and to my friends that which I can only repay by going on the stage."

Early reports indicated that Nan expected to remain at her parents' home in Washington for "some time" as she recuperated from over 11 months of incarceration in the Tombs and, noted a journalist; "the fresh young face and graceful figure little show the traces of that confinement with a life at stake and in the hands of twelve men twice." And, added the report; "Not a visitor who called at the house but failed to comment favorably on her appearance, and the utter absence of anything in her face that would indicate her likelihood of having taken a human life She does not look the part of a murderess, but rather that of a young girl, care-free and innocent of guile." Nan was estimated herein to be 5' 4" in height and to weigh 135 pounds. There had been literally hundreds of people coming to the house in Washington to see Nan, but most did not gain admittance. She did, however, pose for pictures for a reporter with one of the nation's capital daily newspapers. That description of Nan went as follows; "She appears to be a young woman who likes the good things of life and would get them in an easy manner. She was never made for toil and could not long endure a life of privation. Her hands are soft and her figure lissome; neither were made for fighting with the world and it is safe to say that whatever she may elect to do for a living in the future it will be an occupation that will call for a minimum of labor at a maximum reward." And that; "She has not the face that tells of nerve enough to take her own life, yet during the trial she displayed a nerve that was the wonder and admiration of thousands." [Yet during the trials this newspaper, and many others, continuously depicted her as overemotional, hysterical, prone to fainting and swooning, and so forth]. On the evening of Saturday May 13 Nan, the Smiths, and one other person visited several of the "more prominent cafes" of Washington; "At all of them there were persons who recognized the young woman whose face has become familiar to the public, and many craned necks rewarded the visitors while comments of critical and other character greeted their ears." [That indicated that not all reaction to Patterson consisted of cheering and adoring crowds, as was often implied from the media coverage].

Justice Vernon M. Davis of the New York State Supreme Court was the guest of honor on the evening of May 15 at the monthly dinner of the Phi Delta Phi Club, an organization of lawyers in New York City. He presided at the first two trials of Patterson and, to the surprise of some lawyers at the dinner, in his remarks to the group Davis gave his opinion on the guilt of Nan, saying in part; "We have heard a great deal in the public press of late of severe criticism of Mr. Rand and his conduct of the trial." Praising Rand as the second most eloquent prosecutor he had ever heard he added; "You can't prosecute a criminal without telling what you believe to be the truth…In the second trial before me the defendant went on the stand, and it was quite obvious that she was telling falsehoods from beginning to the end. The very air seemed charged with the fact that she was lying. Yet she was a woman. She was young. It was natural that the public should sympathize with her. People seemed to know that she was not telling the truth, and the great public of New York said: 'Why shouldn't she lie? Let her lie. Let her get the benefit of her lies.'"

Then Davis moved on to the final trial, saying; "But to-day, in the light of the last disagreement, I feel sure that most people are convinced that a majority of the people believe that the pistol that killed Caesar Young was held by Nan Patterson, was discharged by her, was bought by J. Morgan Smith in an attempt to get money from Caesar Young for the support of the combined family. I don't mean to say that she took the pistol from the reticule [drawstring purse] and shot him in the side, but I do believe that she had the pistol and showed it to Caesar Young. An argument followed, and he took hold of it. In the conversation and subsequent struggle the pistol went off and the man was killed." One of Nan's lawyers, Daniel O'Reilly commented there was nothing to warrant Davis making such a statement. Nan was on the stand and Rand cross-examined her for one whole day; "She was not contradicted in one statement." If she had lied all the time, wondered O'Reilly, why didn't Rand contradict her testimony.

Such outrageous remarks, as might have been expected, drew comment. A long letter-to-the-editor published in a New York City newspaper remarked; "The trial of Nan Patterson is not an isolated instance of the gross over trying of such cases For years that fault has been the subject of adverse comment among members of the bar and thoughtful people generally, and more especially among the Judges of our Appellate courts." One example cited herein of wrongdoing on the part of the prosecution related to the Smiths. Wherein the District Attorney told the Ohio officials that they had ample evidence of conspiracy and the object of extradition was to undertake "a bona fide effort" to try them for conspiracy. But there was no evidence at all and when a judge dismissed the indictment he said it was totally unwarranted.

A day or two after his remarks, Davis declared he had nothing to take from or add to the speech he made to that gathering of mostly lawyers. When Davis made that speech he made no suggestion that the contents should not become public. Commented Recorder Goff; "I have not read what Justice Davis said and it would make no difference if I had. I make it a practice never to discuss cases that are tried in my court." Neither Rand, nor Jerome, nor Levy would discuss the speech. Not so reticent was Daniel O'Reilly, who stated; "If Justice Davis is justified in his conclusions it only goes to show that the prosecution failed to impress those points on the jury." Said ex-Assistant District Attorney McIntyre; "I cannot commend too highly the courageous and proper stand taken by Mr. Justice Davis...He expressed himself fearlessly as a citizen and was perfectly justified in what he said. I agree with every word spoken by Justice Davis and I commend him again for his courage in so expressing his opinion." McIntyre added; "I approve of the entire course pursued by Mr. Rand...His prosecution of the woman was fair, vigorous and honest. I admire Mr. Rand for his courage, honesty and ability."

One more day later and it developed that more sensational than his remarks about Nan Patterson was Davis' "general condemnation of the methods of lawyers defending criminals" which was part of the remarks he made at that dinner gathering. He plainly said that the legal intelligence and training of the members of the criminal bar were of a lower order than the standard civil practice required He regretted a growing tendency on the part of lawyers engaged in the defense of criminals to try their cases according to "the law of human sympathy." Larger financial returns in civil practice meant, he argued, the attraction of the best legal minds. Justice Charles F. MacLean of the New York Supreme Court said, regarding the remarks by Davis about Nan; "Justice Davis's remarks are eminently proper, in my judgment, and ought to stem the tide of talk in this woman's favor." His only complaint was that such utterances were privileged and should not have been repeated. On May 18 Justice Davis stated; "I have no desire to repeat my speech now. I do not wish to answer questions nor make explanation regarding any part of my address.

Leon Berg was a representative of Hurtig and Seamon, New York theatrical managers and he said on May 13 that his firm had secured a two-year contract with Nan for her appearance in a few weeks in their theater in New York City and later with one of their road companies. Berg said that the contract provided for a sliding scale of remuneration beginning very high and tapering down as public curiosity lessened. Her salary at first, explained Berg, would be about $1,800 a week, which would be for several weeks. An authorized announcement of vehicles she was to appear in would be issued in a few days time, from the office of her counsel Abraham Levy. Purportedly, she also had a contract for a book deal and; "The royalty from the sale of her book will be considerable unless it is too long withheld" No book every did appear.

Two days later Nan went too Philadelphia where it was reported that she signed a contract with Hurtig and Seamon at an alleged salary of $2,000 a week. She was to be the lead player, with six girls, in a vaudeville act. Nan said; "I was in hopes I would not have to return to the stage. I had not been back home long, though, before I realized I must do something. I am a poor girl and my father is so broken in health that he won't be able to work again for some time." And, she continued; "I long for quiet, but it became a question of money, and I have not the training to go into an office or do anything like that. I therefore felt obliged to take advantage of the good offer that was made to me. I was sadly surprised today about what Justice Davis said."

The next day a reporter wrote, with respect to the Hurtig and Seamon contract, that Patterson's first appearance would be on the following Sunday evening [May 21] at a "sacred concert." The salary agreed on under the contract was $3,000 for one week and if she "makes good" the contract would be made for one year at $1,500 a week and a certain percentage of the gross receipts. Nan would sing three songs and have as a chorus "pretty maidens," numbering, in this piece, eight females. While she was in Philadelphia supposedly finalizing the deal she also met in that city with her lawyers so they might arrange to get part of the proceeds from that contract, to go towards paying the legal bills that she had amassed. Nan was expected to leave Washington for New York City for rehearsals and to have costumes made at an expense of $500 each, with two slated to be made. Her act would last for 20 minutes and it was expected to include some of the songs she sang in *Floradora.* All the time that she was traveling she was accompanied by her other sister, Mrs. Harriet Lowell. If at all went well, Patterson was said to have hopes of realizing about $50,000 from the contract that she has just signed.

While the above reports seemed to have been accurate and final, that was not the case. It was suddenly announced that the statements that Nan had signed a contract with Hurtig and Seamon to appear in New York City in vaudeville the following week were not true. Those statements were denied on May 17 by one of her lawyers, Daniel O'Reilly. He told the press that while his client had gone to Philadelphia especially for a conference with the theatrical managers, she had refused their offer for an immediate engagement. "It is true that Miss Patterson was offered $2,000 a week by Hurtig and Seamon to sing a few songs with a chorus accompaniment. She went with me to Philadelphia yesterday to talk the matter over and decided not to accept," explained O'Reilly. "Miss Patterson feels that it is too soon for her to appear before the public in that capacity. Some time later she will probably accept such an offer, but so far there is no contract nor any definite understanding about an arrangement being made in the future." The lawyer continued; "Nan has no desire to figure longer in the public eye. Moreover in view of what was said by the girl in all sincerity about her wish to go home and stay there as soon as her freedom was obtained, she could not appear upon the stage now without incurring severe censure. The offer, nevertheless is a tempting one." Hurtig and Seamon issued a comment around the same time that while business negotiations with Nan had been pending they had no definite statement to make.

A different account of the same meeting between Nan and the theatrical managers and Daniel O'Reilly, cited the lawyer as having something different to say. "The girl must go on the stage as soon as possible while the general interest in her personality is at its height. It's a necessity in her case. What else can she do? Not only is she without means, but she has large financial obligations to meet." One of her other lawyers, Abraham Levy, disclaimed any knowledge of her plans. He said; "With Miss Patterson's discharge and return to her family my connection with her case ended. If she goes on the stage it will be against my advice. But that is her own affair."

Then there was a seeming reversal, of sorts. On May 18 it was announced that Nan was holding a "secret audience" that day "with a skilled army of dressmakers, lingerie artists, milliners and feminine haberdashers in preparation for the most elaborate outfit that a chorus girl has ever possessed." When she made her vaudeville debut "week after next" she would have "besides a pretty face, something to show that will atone for her inability to either sing or dance. According to this piece Nan's much talked of engagement with Hurtig and Seamon "is practically closed. The contract will not be signed until to-morrow, but the girl has verbally accepted an offer to sing a few songs, with a background of pretty chorus girls, for a salary of $2,000 a week." Her opening was then said to be scheduled for Monday May 30 in the Hurtig and Seamon theater in Harlem, New York.

In unrelated news, Mrs. Frank Thomas Young (Margaret) sailed for Liverpool, around that time, on the White Star liner Majestic, under the name of Mrs. Jacob Becker. John Millin accompanied her and sailed under the name of John Becker. Rumor had it that the pair were to be married. Millin tried to hide his identity, but he was spotted by some of the people on the pier. Bernard S. McKean, brother-in-law of Caesar, denied any marriage plans and explained that Millin had gone on the voyage with Margaret and her mother as an escort.

A lawyer by the name of C. A. Irwin was "reported to be a leading member of the bar at Sioux City Iowa," was circulating the story that Abraham Levy had told him that Nan Patterson had privately confessed to Levy that she held the weapon that killed Young. It was all more nonsense as attempts by people trying to gain publicity, but who had nothing to do with the case, seemed to be never ending. Said Levy, when told of the story; "I don't know Mr. Irwin. I have never seen him, I have never been to Sioux City...Irwin's statement is a barefaced lie."

While a book by Nan Patterson about her experiences never did emerge she had at least one or two articles published, under her byline, although there were probably written by ghost-writers. One appeared on May 18 and was fairly lengthy. It appeared in a number of newspapers and was signed by her with her literal signature appearing with the piece. It was titled; "Warning to girls." Nan was said to have written the piece in her cell at the Tombs during her last week of incarceration there. It was touted as "the only authorized statement Miss Patterson has made for any newspaper." The copyright holder was the press syndicate Newspaper Enterprise Association. A subhead of the piece proclaimed that she "writes in strong earnest words of dangers which beset young women and cautions of dangers to be avoided" Starting with a reminder to the reader that she was just finishing a year of incarceration, minus 23 days, she explained her reasons for writing the piece by stating that because of the "torture unspeakable" that she had just endured; "I feel that it is right that I should say a word now to the thousands of high-spirited American girls who are just peeping in the alluring image of stage life, and the hot, fast pace of modern, useless living." Nan explained that she knew what it was to be headstrong and self-willed and to refuse to listen to the warning words of her best friends; "I would not attempt to condemn the stage, but I do most sincerely condemn the temptations which go with it." She went on to write; "My first great misstep came when I fell in love with a married man...I lost the finer sensibilities through my mad infatuation. No good could come from it. No good can come to it for any one. Look at what I have suffered for my mistake...I warn all against the so-called fascination of the race track life, and all that pertains to it. I warn them against idleness, fast living, restaurant life, drink. These can bring naught but unhappiness and misery."

The most interesting part of her article was her description of her life in the Tombs. Nan explained that women prisoners there were not separated during the day from 6:00 AM to 4:00 PM, but only at night when each was locked in a narrow cell about four feet wide by 10 feet long in which the only furnishings consisted of a narrow iron cot, stretched across in lieu of springs was a heavy canvas secured to the framework by ropes. To each prisoner was allotted two sheets of coarse linen, two gray blankets, one to be used in place of a mattress, the other as a cover, a gingham spread of blue and white check and a hard, narrow pillow of straw. Except for those cots the cells were bare. About 6:00 AM the prisoner was awakened and then they made their way to the pen. Into that pen, a narrow corridor not more than eight feet wide and almost four times as long, were crowded the constantly changing numbers of female detainees, as many as 20 or even more. From six in the morning until four in the afternoon all of those varied women were penned together.

Several days later it was reported that Nan had returned to New York City and had begun the new life of which she spoke while in her call at the Tombs. She began that existence, noted a journalist sarcastically; "by visiting Broadway restaurants in an automobile with a merry party." Nan's chaperon remained her sister Mrs. Harriet C. Lowell. This account mentioned her Hurtig and Seamon contract and that it contained "most unusual stipulations". They are in the nature of pledges of her good behavior for a year." She had agreed, over her signature, not to drink any intoxicating liquors for one year, not to visit any saloons or cafes where liquor is sold during that one year period and never to appear upon the public streets without a chaperon. According to this account these "unusual restrictions" were placed in the contracts of Nan because of the experience which Harry Seamon had on the night Nan was liberated from the Tombs. However, that experience was not elaborated. According to this account's version of her contract she was to receive $2,000 from Hurtig and Seamon for the first week and her compensation thereafter was to depend on the success of her first week's performance. It was agreed Harriet Lowell would be acceptable to all parties as a suitable chaperon. She was a resident of Washington D. C., and ran a little store there that sold small articles in the government buildings to help raise money for Nan while she was incarcerated. This version also mentioned that Nan was to write a book and magazine articles. It was said herein that Nan consented to go on the stage in order to raise money to settle with Abraham Levy who had defended her without pay. Levy, however, had said he would not accept any money for his services which might be raised by his client in that way. Levy exclaimed; "I disapprove of all that Nan Patterson has done since she left the Tombs. I want no girl to work to pay my fee, and what I have done for this girl stands on record as having been done without compensation."

Another long article abut Patterson appeared, on May 25, and was also reprinted in various newspapers. It was supposedly her story but she did not receive a byline in the piece. In this version Nan met Caesar on the train going to California in July 1902. She was an actor and had been with a *Floradora* company in the early part of the season and later with the stage production *A Chinese Honeymoon*. Having received an offer to join a stock company in Los Angeles she resigned from *A Chinese Honeymoon* and was on her way on the train to take the new engagement.. She soon began an affair with Young. She was married to Leon Martin in Baltimore when she was just 16 but when she met Caesar she was already separated; "I knew that Mr. Young was married, for he told me so." As a result of the meeting she did not go to Los Angeles but stayed with Young during the racing season. Young suggested Nan divorce and she did, in San Francisco, in May 1903. Leaving the west coast she came east in March 1904 and had been in New York for only two weeks when Young telegraphed her to come back to San Francisco, and she did so. Nan met Julia's husband Morgan Smith for the first time during that time in New York City. When she returned to the west coast she met Caesar in Los Angeles in the middle of April. Soon thereafter the pair returned to San Francisco as Mrs. Young had arrived there. Next they went east but on separate trains meeting, as agreed, in Chicago. Later separate trains carried Nan to Washington and Caesar to New York City. Around the start of May, she said, Margaret Young began to suspect the couple. She then repeated much of the material for late May and early June, often covered in the past. This piece seemed to mostly appear in small newspapers with the larger ones, perhaps, having already featured most of the contained material.

Despite all the confusing reports about Patterson and her on again off again return to the stage she was definitely going to appear on the stage. The managers of the woman announced that she would appear at the Manhattan Beach Theatre in Denver in her tour of the west. And that bothered some. A report from Denver Colorado on May 23 came in the form of an announcement from the manager of that venue in Denver. He said he would not allow her to appear on the stage at his venue. He was quoted as saying that Nan was only a $20-a-week chorus girl prior to the death of Young and that she was worth no more than that currently.

The next chapter in Nan's saga to return to the stage took place in Wilkes-Barre Pennsylvania where it was announced, near the end of May, that Nan was to appear in that city as the star of the stage production "A Romance in Panama," in both the matinee and evening performances scheduled for Tuesday May 30 in that city. That announcement provoked "numerous indignant protests" to city officials. Wilkes-Barre Mayor E. C. Kirkendall received a score or more appeals "from ministers and prominent ladies" asking him to use his best endeavors to prevent the performances from happening. They declared that the "parading" of Patterson so soon after her release "in view of the fact that all of the world knows what kind of life she led, is indecent and improper. Nan was booked there under the management of George Harris, with the production being a musical comedy and containing a cast of 40 players.

Mayor Kirkendall, "despite the appeals of more than a hundred prominent citizens," most of them steady patrons of the theater, found it would be impossible for him to prevent the appearance on May 30. After a consultation with attorneys he found he could not legally suppress the performance and on the morning of May 28 he appealed to Harry Brown manager of the venue, the Nesbitt Theater, and laid before him the protests of the people who had called on him. Brown assured him there was nothing objectionable in the performance and that as the production had been booked by his New York agents and the contract signed he could not refuse to allow Nan to appear. A number of women of the community were then trying to get together a large committee to make a personal appeal to the managers to halt the performance "on behalf of all the better class of theatergoers in this city" Those women contended that harm would be done to the many "silly girls" who looked upon Nan as a heroine.

More drama unfolded as Nan was about to begin her matinee performance on May 30 in Wilkes-Barre and was served with an injunction restraining her from appearing. The injunction was granted on the application of Irving Pinover, who said she broke a contract signed with him as her manager. Reportedly, though, she did appear there for the evening performance. She came on stage for her song a few minutes before the curtain fell in the last act. Nan was unannounced but the audience recognized her and "applauded vigorously...She sang in a weak little voice, and was called out three times."

When Nan was scheduled to appear at the Lyceum Theatre in Scranton Pennsylvania on the evening of May 29 a reporter stated, that afternoon, that it was expected to be greeted by one of the biggest crowds in the history of the house. Reportedly, there was a great demand for seats and only a few remained unsold. No formal protest has been made with regard to the appearance of Patterson. She arrived in Scranton at 2:00 PM that day and, said the journalist; "Much interest had been aroused and there were big crowds abut the station and hotel anxious to get a glimpse of her."

An editorial about Nan Patterson's attempts to launch her

return to the stage, appeared on the last day of May. The editor began by mentioning the Denver venue manager and went on to conclude; "The manager has some pride in his house." Continued the editor; "There is a big difference between fame and notoriety though the two are frequently confused in some minds. The public does not always distinguish...Billing her as a star does not increase her merit...But in those play houses where money is the only object Nan Patterson will draw better audiences than the most accomplished woman of the stage. Curiosity will open the pocketbooks. Nan will be counted as a success." That editor concluded by stating; "There are many right thinking people, however, who tire of seeing this crude creature posing under the lime light. In view of her career modest subsidence would much become her. Nan Patterson's disappearance is long overdue."

Several days later a different editorial writer on the same topic declared; "The revolt of the people of those towns where theatrical engagements have been made for Nan Patterson's appearance behind the footlights, is a reassuring sign of an awakening public sense of the proprieties and will be applauded by all who desire the suppression of such exhibitions upon the stage of the country." The prompt refusal of the people of Wilkes-Barre "sounded the key-note of this manifestation of disapproval, and there are not lacking indications that there will be a similar repugnance on the part of theatre-goers in other cities and towns embraced on her proposed tour...It would be a good thing indeed for public morals and self respect if this woman should be refused recognition everywhere and her pilgrimage in quest of dollars be therefore made the failure it deserves to be." In conclusion, this editor added; "This country has had quite enough of Nan Patterson, through causes it could not well control, without voluntarily perpetuating her reign as a celebrity by compensation."

On the evening of June 5 in Altoona Pennsylvania Nan Patterson severed her connection with *The Romance of Panama* theater company and left for her home in Washington. Reportedly she had become discouraged by the adverse criticism that had greeted her re-appearance on the stage and she was "broken in spirit and disheartened." Nan was greeted by a "small house" in Altoona on Saturday night [June 3] and "the few women present [in the audience] left early." As she was boarding the train later in the evening to go home to Washington she told reporters; "When I went on the stage I adopted the only means left to me to earn a livelihood, and I am awfully sorry the people have so severely condemned me. I wanted to do right, and could see no harm in going on the stage, which is my profession. I owe thousands of dollars and don't know how in the world I am going to pay it in any other way." She added that; "rather than bear the harsh treatment that I have been subjected to, I have decided to leave the stage, for a time at least."

An opinion piece in a western paper, on the drama and amusements page remarked that the fact that Nan's tour had come to a halt because of her failure to draw a reasonably-sized audience was "not the least gratifying view of theatrical news received last week...Decent folk in and out of the profession have no sympathy to bestow on Miss Patterson's manager, who lost a tidy sum by underestimating the American public's intelligence and sense of propriety." And, concluded the piece; "Nan's failure to attract serves to show that the mob, always ready to rush to see the vulgar or notorious has the redeeming quality of curbing its curiosity, when the magnet combines suspected assassinations with lewdness of character."

A final editorial on the topic was titled, "An object lesson." It began with an invented, fanciful background for Patterson; "In early girlhood she made her debut on the stage behind the footlights. She at once became a favorite of theatre-goers. Her picture appeared in all the illustrated magazines and newspapers. She rose to the zenith of the theatrical world. While thus gaining fame and fortune her downfall came. The public is familiar with all that has followed." Of course, none of that background was true, or even had a small element of truth in it. However, the theme of the editorial was along the lines of how the mighty have fallen. And that meant, apparently, that a faked huge fame had to be created, since a real one had not existed. Nan had a role of no great length or importance in a popular stage production and appeared on the stage for perhaps less than two years, with very little notice taken of her during that time. She performed briefly and competently during that stage career but gained no notice or attention. After creating the fake past the editor said; "Nan Paterson was freed, without proof of her guilt or innocence of an awful crime...But a dark cloud hovers over her. That she has been punished no one can gainsay, but there still remains an unforgiving public." Nan went home, briefly, but could not adjust to it; "A deeper shadow has fallen upon the unfortunate girl than upon her home, and has fallen upon her by her own sin...No penalty is so sure as that which comes with the suicide of sin...Nan Patterson can return to her old home but a cloud will ever hang over it. Her innocence of childhood cannot return." Naturally, thought the editor, she sought remunerative employment; "but in her anxiety the attempt is made too soon. She does not receive the plaudits of old, but in their stead a cold unchristian greeting..." Concluded the editor; "Let the young man and young woman learn an object lesson from the sorrows that have overtaken Miss Patterson."

A long, two-page article appeared in the middle of June that presented itself as a think piece reflecting on the Patterson case. The title of the piece was; "Does it pay to be good?" while a sub-head proclaimed; "Wide echoes of the Nan Patterson case in the world of women – answers to the question by thinkers and workers in New York. The real prizes for the good girl – the hard way of the transgressor." More than any other article on the subject, this one captured the real focus of the negative coverage and the smear pieces about Nan. This was blatantly and openly misogynistic and opposed to any type of equality for females. For the author of this piece it was clear that Nan was evil, guilty of great sin and deserving of punishment – and not for the death of Young. The piece began by pointing out that a short time ago a 22-year-old girl was on trial for her life and; "The evidence brought forth by the state clearly showed that this girl had run the gamut of every crime, due to the degradation of womanhood. She had been married and divorced. She had been a *Floradora* chorus girl. She had been a vampire [seductress] to a bookmaker, a married man. She and her sister and her sister's husband had obtained large sums of money from this man with whom she had consorted in open shame." It went on to outline briefly the hansom cab ride, the trials, the big salary of $2,000 a week to return to the stage and; "Then the reaction came. The shop girls and factory hands, the stenographers and those drudging daily for a bare pittance, read, pondered and then questioned: 'Does it pay to be good?'" Apparently that question led to this article as a response. Women were cautioned if they had contrasted their hard work, small wages, monotonous lives against that glamour – then those girls were advised to walk through Madison Square [well-known for prostitutes plying their trade], or to check out the opium dens in Chinatown and so on, for the women in those latter two places were once the same as the hard-working girls mentioned earlier; "A woman prospering in wickedness is so exceptional that she stands out like a clear cut cameo. This ill gotten luxury and easy living rarely go with her to the grave." This piece was likely written before Nan's stage comeback fizzled out and it went on to note that soon the limelight of publicity would fall from her; "and she will be cast aside as of no further use, a victim to liquor and drugs, saturated in vice, a poor, singed moth, vainly bating against the bulb which encloses her flame, and will finally sink to the ground and die."

Then the piece published comments on the central question as to whether or not it paid to be good, for a woman. The five individuals were all named; they were all men. Isidor Straus commented; "True, her present success is bewildering, but we must not judge an apple by its outward appearance. How many rosy cheeked apples when we cut into them are found rotten at the core?" James Hamilton (of the University Settlement) asserted; "There is hope even for Nan Patterson could she once taste the joy of humble serving." Robert C. Ogden insisted that since he was interested in the employment of women that he should not appear before the public as expressing opinions upon the subject involved. Lieutenant-Colonel William H. Cox (Salvation Army) stated; "The testimony of the girls themselves demonstrates it does pay to be good." The male Superintendent of Bellevue Hospital provided figures on alcoholism among women; "Women of the class of Nan Patterson, suffering from diseases brought on by dissipation and neglect, are brought to the hospital...Nine out of every ten, their condition being so serious die, while those having any chance to live are sent to [the poorhouse at] Randall's Island.

A long short story, or perhaps a novella, "written by Nan Patterson was serialized in the New York City newspaper the *World* in June 1905. It was a work of fiction that had nothing to do with the Patterson case. Chapter five, for example, appeared in print on June 29. A brief summary preceded the chapter, giving a synopsis of the first four chapter. It went as follows; "Rex Venner, department superintendent of Rother's jewelry store, exhibits the Belgrade diamonds (two jewels of fabulous value) to Amy Clare, his fiance. Charles Beckwith, a famous detective, for whom Amy works as a stenographer, and Mme Delorme, the beautiful widow of a South American republic's President, are also present. The Belgrade diamonds are stolen and Rex is arrested, charged with the theft. Amy has reason to believe that Mme. Delorme has stolen the diamonds, but an interview with her brings no results. Amy then visits Rex in the Tombs and tells him of an amazing plan for his relief." While Patterson is giving the author byline for this effort it was not likely written by her.

In spite of the admonition from Recorder Goff to keep away from her old life Nan, according to one report, a little after two months of freedom, had returned to the racetrack. According to the story she was recognized by some people at the track, in late July and was greeted. Nan was described as having made a $10 bet and when she lost "pouted in disappointment." It was also said that; "Nan seemed to enjoy the notoriety and she walked around the grand stand before she went to the dining room where she imbibed several glasses of champagne. After a dinner at the hotel she was with a party of men who occupied a conspicuous box at a roof garden and she seemed to enjoy the curiosity she aroused in the audience as much as the show."

When an editor looked at "Nan Patterson again" at the beginning of August 1905 he offered the opinion that she had been freed after trial number three and not retried because a message of charity and forgiveness was delivered to the woman – it was a message saying; "Go and sin no more." Then Nan went to her family home in Washington D. C., but did not stay there; "She reappeared behind the footlights. There was silent resentment. The seats in the box offices remained unsold and then – Broadway knew Nan Patterson again. Again was she seen in the glittering restaurants. Again did she pass down the avenues in hansom cabs. Thursday and Friday has found her on the race track, smiling boldly at the starers, gambling on the races and seemingly wholly unmindful that the race track was the scene of one of the sordid chapters in the Young tragedy." Continuing on the editor added; "Far be it for me to cast a stone at any woman, but this much is justly said: Nan Patterson on the race track in gowns that her white-haired father could not have purchased for her; Nan Patterson gambling; Nan Patterson back in the old garish tinsel resorts, in the doing of these things Nan Patterson is dealing a stinging blow of ingratitude into the faces of the good women, pure and kindly women, merciful men and unstained girls, who believing in her inherent goodness, in their anxiety to see her restored to her home and parents, poured out their sympathy to her in prayers, in letters, in telegrams, and through the press, creating that expression of public will, 'Go and sin no more' which set her free."

A few days later another editor remarked that; "Nan Patterson has gone back to the race track and the lobster palaces of Broadway and the jockeys and the Johnnies [stage door Johnnies were sexual harassers and predators of the era who hung around stage doors of an evening when plays finished. They hoped to corral female players as they exited from the theatre]. Already she is condemned for it. But is it fair? What can she do?" Said the editor; "She has no trade – but the sad old first trade of women, to which the signs are she is returning. It's all very fine to sneer at Nan's repentance – but the woman must live…It's hard to be decent and pinched, when you've lived in the lights and the music, on fine viands and exalted wines, when one is young." As far as this editor was concerned; "She is a symptom of economic disease. She is a part of the great, universal, ever-pressing bread-and-butter question, even more than she is, as Lecky said, a priestess of humanity blasted for the sins of the people." Why did they need the money, the editor mused rhetorically; "Because if you get not money you are crushed to earth, and the masters walk over you, if they cannot use you or you can't amuse them…but she is inescapable in any age or part of the world where money has sway; she is the first and smallest sacrifice, in all her joy, to the greed that poisons all the sweetness and plenty of life."

Troubles continued to dog Nan, who was living in New York City in the summer of 1905. On August 15 she packed her belongings hurriedly and gave up her apartments at the Cambridge Court Hotel on 49th Street near Seventh Avenue. She left word for any callers that she had gone to Washington D. C. At the same time a statement was issued by Mrs. V. D. Handy (New York City) alleging Patterson had been "altogether too friendly" with her brother-in-law C. Ralph Ash, a well-to-do lumber broker of Duluth Minnesota. Twice Mrs. Handy had tried to have an "interview" with Nan but failed each time. Said Handy; "I would like to meet that woman in a dark street and while I know my position, I feel that a mix-up and blackened eyes might result." Reportedly, Nan had recently told friends; "I am going to marry Ralph Ash. He has asked me to be his wife, and I have accepted and am going to cut loose from all my old acquaintances and settle down to a quiet domestic life." It turned out that Ash was married and the father of four children.

Nan, it was said, had no idea he was already married. Patterson was registered at the Cambridge Court Hotel as Helen Needham. According to Handy Ash had known Patterson for only four weeks and in that time had gained Broadway notoriety as a "liberal spender." In her own statement Nan declared she did not even know Ash. That statement was released through a friend who accompanied Nan from New York City to Washington, but would not give her name. Meanwhile, in Washington the parents of Patterson both insisted that the trip home by their daughter had been planned for some time.

One day later C. Ralph Ash also left New York City. He left on a train to Duluth as he went home to his wife and children after, said a journalist; "a very determined sister-in-law having secured him from the fascinating wiles of Nan Patterson..." Mrs. Handy declared that in the month Ash saw the woman her brother-in-law threw away a "small fortune" on Nan and her friends. She was first introduced to Ash as Helen Needham but a few days later she told him her real name. A week earlier Handy first learned of the relationship between the pair and remonstrated with Ash. Ralph promised to give up the woman but he did not do so.

Then there unfolded a surprise turn of events. On September 16 1905 at noon in Washington D. C., surrounded by members of her family Ann Elizabeth married her former husband Leon Gaines Martin. Later that day the couple left for New York City. A Congregational minister refused to perform the ceremony, but the knot was tied by Reverend Dudley, rector of St. Stephen's Episcopal Church.

Reverend M. Ross Fishburn of Mt. Pleasant Congregational Church in Washington was the clergyman who refused to conduct the ceremony, while the Reverend George Fiske Dudley was the clergyman who agreed to officiate. Before his first marriage to Nan, Leon was employed in the Pennsylvania Railroad office in Washington D. C. His mother was said to be a wealthy San Francisco woman and one of his brothers, Bert Martin, held a seat on the San Francisco Stock Exchange. The marriage license listed Leon Gaines Martin as 37 and Nan as 23. The ceremony took place at the Patterson family home at 1462 Howard Ave, Northwest. Three of Nan's sisters attended, Mrs. Lowell, Mrs. Taylor, and Mrs. Milburne, along with her brother Charles. The Smiths were not in town at the time of the event. Said John Patterson, Nan's father; "I am very much pleased at the outcome and I trust this action will refute the many scandalous statements, charges, and reports that have been made about my daughter by sensational newspapers, during the trials and after."

Some time later after the couple had taken a honeymoon and settled back into New York City Nan said; "We have returned to take up the simple life. I have abandoned all intention of every resuming a place on the stage. I am devoted to my husband who will go with me immediately to Washington, where we will at least spend one Christmas at home with my mother."

It was announced late in February 1906 that Mrs. Margaret Young spent $4,254 on Caesar Young's burial and a further $3,030 to erect a monument to his memory. More surprising was the extent of the estate of the deceased. It consisted of 100 shares of the California Jockey Club (worth $10,000), and a membership in the Metropolitan Turf Club (valued at $3,000). Thus, his estate was totaled $13,000 in value and he was indebted to his wife for $19,000. After his burial expenses and other debts had been paid Mrs. Young received $6,212, against her claim for $19,000. A bewildered journalist wondered; "What became of the money he used in running his books and the string of horses...does not appear." At the time of his death it was reported in various places that he had been worth $500,000 or more. After the death of her husband Margaret Young selected George W. Langdon to look after his racing stable and other interests. On May 4 1909 Margaret Young married George Langdon.

Some nine months after Nan re-married Leon a long article, illustrated and covering about three-quarters of a page, appeared to update readers on Nan's life. The tone of the article was that

Patterson was a "genuinely reformed woman." A lengthy sub-head exclaimed; "The reckless Floradora girl who danced her way into notoriety and 'went the pace' with the best of them – a pace that eventually landed her in the Tombs on a charge of murder, has completely disappeared and in her stead there rules over a quiet household in the capital a serious modest woman, whose highest condition in life is to make her husband's home all that the word implies." The first sentence of the piece began by stating; "Living quietly in Washington is a new Nan Patterson. For more than 4 months Mrs. Martin has lived in Washington and outside of the friends who stuck with her through think and thin, not a half a dozen persons knew her whereabouts." And, the article continued; "It has been a quiet life after the turmoil of recent years...Nan has known at last the life of a loving wife and the hope of every true woman. For the maternal feeling is strong in woman; it finds a place even in the love which she bestows upon the husband and is responsible for the wealth of tenderness and care which she heaps upon a mere man."

Upon her release from prison, according to this piece, Nan had "according to her own statement, went a pace by which her life previous to her incarceration paled into insignificance." Everything was gone, her parents were heart-broken, her good name was good, the man she loved was dead, the horrors of over 11 months of incarceration were still in her mind – with her home, love and reputation gone, nothing seemed to matter. Someone told her that Margaret Young had erected a monument over her husband's grave and the statute that was a part of that memorial, a figure of any angel with arms outstretched, as if in forgiveness, had, strange to say "a most striking resemblance to Nan Patterson herself." So, telling no one, Nan went to visit the grave to see for herself. She took one look at the memorial and dropped to her knees and said; "There in front of me, pure and cold and white, was my second self...it said to me , 'It is not too late.' I forgot where I was, at whose grave I knelt. I only knew I wanted to be good...I wanted to be as pure and good and as clean and white as the figure above me that seemed to star out of my own face...[I] vowed to God and to myself to try and be a woman." On the day of that "epiphany" she turned to her ex-husband Leon Martin, who had kept in touch with her throughout the period after the separation. After her re-marriage to Martin the couple went to New York City but Nan found she "could not venture out of doors without the publicity which had now become distasteful to her. It was decided, therefore, to establish a permanent home in Washington." Over four month in Washington Patterson was said to have lived the life of a recluse, with the couple residing with one of her sisters and a brother-in-law. Concluded the piece; "That her repentance is complete is shown by the fact that the diamonds she formerly wore, the gifts of Caesar Young, have been stripped from her hands." Reportedly, the one and only cloud on Nan's horizon was that the indictment for murder was still pending over her head. In cases such as this one where the District Attorney did not intend to re-try a case after a hung jury the customary procedure was to quash the indictment after six months. Presumably the delay was to lessen any embarrassment that might have been forthcoming. Six months after the fact there would be little publicity given to the abandonment of an indictment. However, in Nan's case the indictment remained on the books when this article was published, 11 months after Patterson was freed from incarceration.

The above article was the only one that took the stance that Patterson had genuinely reformed. One year later that idea that Nan had "reverted" to her past sinful ways resurfaced again. In a June 14 1907 article that came from Pittsburgh it was observed that; "She again is leading the life she led before her experiences in the Tombs. She was again in the limelight in Pittsburgh even though it was announced that she was going to join her husband in California. Patterson arrived in Pittsburgh a week or so earlier, ostensibly on her way to her husband. When she arrived there she went to a downtown hotel where she registered under an assumed name. But; "Since that time she has been conspicuous in restaurants and cafes when the lights are brightest by night, and she seldom leaves her apartments during the day." With female friends she had been seen constantly in the company of two young men of Pittsburgh, (one was married) at prominent cafes where they stayed until closing. Patterson had arrived in that Pennsylvania city on June 7 or June 8 and the description of her time there related to Friday June 14. On Wednesday night (June 12) she went to the apartment of a woman friend at the Duquesne Hotel and ordered wine sent to the room; "but the management refused to sell her anything and instructed the clerks to send nothing to her." Reportedly, Leon Martin was in the West, waiting for Nan to join in there. When he left it was announced that she was going with him but instead, it was said, she went to her old home in Washington.

An editorial about the revelations of Nan in Pittsburgh and that she was "leading the old life" there, appeared a number of days later. The editor argued that before Nan figured in the Young shooting "her shame had not been generally proclaimed to the world...but in the tenderloin districts of many cities she was known as a painted Jezebel. She was the companion of sports and rounders. She lived where the glasses clinked and the ribald song rang loudly. She had no gift of mind or attribute of character to recommend her. Even her voice was of indifferent quality." And; "A pretty face and figure formed her sole appeal, and that appeal, naturally, went to the baser elements of society. Those few decent people who knew her wretched story were perhaps appropriately shocked." But when the woman came "demurely" into a court of justice "modestly" dressed "good people in every State in the Union became her partisans. They invited many of them upon her innocence...Public clamor was on her side through three trials and finally she went unwhipped by justice. This editor concluded by remarking; "The shallowness of her pretense to a restored virtue and a renewed chastity was indicated when she quickly renounced her expressed intention to devote her life to useful labor. She took to the vaudeville stage in the hope of reaping a fortune – merely by permitting herself to be looked at. But public interest turned to popular disgust, and her venture fall flat."

Another report from Pittsburgh, on July 1, declared that Nan was still leading the wild life in Pittsburgh although; "some of her friends are making an effort to get the unfortunate girl on her feet and have her continue on her way to Los Angeles to the bedside of her dying husband." Reportedly, Patterson was spending much of her time at a roadhouse and most of her time there "in the barroom, leaning up against the rail and is frequently the only woman among a roomful of men."

A few days after that an editor with a Kansas newspaper briefly recapped Patterson's story after her release, her promise to do better, her failing on her stage career comeback, then she sought oblivion with her husband but she was not able to put behind her the longings for her old life. "She has the same old heart – the heart whose wickedness had led her to become the mistress of Caesar Young and had plunged her into untold depths of trouble," declared the editor. Recently she appeared in Pittsburgh where she said she was just spending a few hours to change trains as she hurried to Los Angeles "where her husband lay sick. Temptation came to her in that brief interval and she forgot her sick husband." He concluded by noting; "It is difficult to overlook the fall of Nan Patterson because she is a woman – and more is expected of women than of men – because she passed through a severe lesson, and because of her protestations of reform...The best plan is not to go wrong in the first place."

At the end of August it was reported that for the past six weeks Nan had been showing Pittsburgh residents "how they burn the candle at both ends in New York," but that she had suddenly disappeared from her old haunts in that city. At around the same time a wealthy Pittsburgh steel man, who had been her companion, went to a private sanitarium, suffering from "nervous prostration." His relatives, who it was said, were responsible for Nan's departure "are much relieved" in spirit. It was believed then that Patterson had left Pittsburgh for Washington. Her husband Leon Martin was said to be in Los Angeles.

Back in Washington Nan responded to rumors that he husband Leon was going to divorce here by saying such speculation was untrue. That the only reason she had not gone to Los Angeles to join her husband was that Leon had not been well lately and thus he could not work. As soon as he got work, she explained, she planned to join him there. That is, when he was earning enough to support both of them. Nan was then living with her parents. The stories emanating from Pittsburgh were characterized by her as false; "As for the wine suppers, well, about the strongest thing I have had to drink this summer has been ice cream soda." As well, she insisted she did not know any men in Pittsburgh in the steel industry. Even then, over 15 months after her release from incarceration the murder indictment against the young woman had not been quashed and remained over her head. Nan declared that it "has been held as a means of insuring a quiet life" on her part. There was a fear that Jerome would retry her if he heard of bad behavior on her part. Said Nan; "From the way they talk and write about me, there is no incentive to try and do what is right, for I appear to get the worst of it, anyway."

Then, at the beginning of September a new story surfaced about her time in Pittsburgh. According to this tale about six months earlier Dr. John Brittyn, a successful and high-priced masseur in that city met Patterson at a roadhouse and became infatuated with the "former chorus girl." His attentions became pronounced and when Nan gave him up for the Pittsburgh steel man – who, it was declared, she threatened a few weeks earlier to kill with her hatpin – the masseur was heartbroken. After she transferred her affections to the steel man the doctor became morose and depressed. Soon thereafter he went to St. Louis and on September 1 came the news that on August 29 he committed suicide by hanging himself. When confronted with that tale Nan stated; "As God is my judge, I never heard of nor saw the Pittsburgh masseur that they say killed himself for love of me." And, she added; "Yesterday it was a Pittsburgh steel man, today it is a masseur, and tomorrow it will probably be some one else, and there is just as little truth in one story as another. And I and my family have to suffer, just the same. All this talk and these vicious reports are making a nervous wreck of me, and slowly but surely killing my mother."

In a different report on Brittyn it was said that he and Nan had spent days together at the Wildwood Inn, a roadhouse in Pittsburgh with the result that Brittyn neglected his business and spent all his money in company with Nan "who is still unacquitted of the murder of Caesar Young." Brittyn was not wealthy and soon spent all the money he had saved. When Brittyn was running out of money Patterson "turned her attention to men who were more prosperous. In vain Brittyn attempted to retain favor It is said he was repeatedly rebuffed, and that finally the woman had openly insulted him and commanded him never to speak to her again."

A full year passed with Nan continuing to reside in Pittsburgh. Then she left Pittsburgh on the afternoon of July 25 1908, for parts unknown, after having a conference with the police officials in that city. Speaking of the matter a day or so later Pittsburgh Police Department Captain of Detectives Roach declared; "when I told her she would have to go she agreed to do so. The wife of a prominent man called up on the telephone stating that Nan Patterson had enticed her husband, and Nan Patterson admitted this, promising to leave the city at once."

A different account of the Pittsburgh police episode started with a brief recap of the Young case and a few statements from Nan that she had made in the past, about reforming and avoiding the wild life, and so on. Then it invented conversations between Patterson and Roach. Said Roach to Nan, in these manufactured remarks; "There is no alternative! You have had your chance. Leave Pittsburgh before 12 tonight, or the police will send you to the workhouse for vagrancy...I don't care where you go, only you can't wreak any more homes in Pittsburgh." Then this account added that; "The extravagantly dressed young woman rose impatiently."

The next time Nan surfaced in the media was in late April

1909 when it was remarked that discovery had just been made of the fact that the strange woman who had been making frequent visits to the Emergency Hospital to see F. Bernard Stevens, who was mysteriously shot on the night of April 24 while in the United States Savings Bank with J. M. Boker Jr., was Nan. She was then living with her parents at the Berwyn Apartments, which were within a few yards of the United States Savings Bank. Stevens, who was the assistant cashier of the bank had been boarding with the Pattersons. Apparently the media was trying to tie Patterson in with that holdup and shooting at the bank but nothing came of it. It did, however, give a glimpse into the life of Nan. The family had always lived in their own house but at this time were reduced to apartment renting. Also they had a boarder living with them within that apartment, perhaps.

One curiosity, indirectly connected to the Patterson case, emerged in November 1910. At that time Edward T. Rosenheimer, a millionaire, was on trial for the alleged murder of Grace Hough, by running her down with his automobile. George W. Yeandle, an architect, who had been selected as juror number nine for that trial was arrested on November 1 for bribery. Yeandle used an intermediary by the name of Dagobert Timondoffer who approached James W. Osborne, lawyer for Rosenheimer. The latter told Osborne that Yeandle was responsible for the hung jury in the Patterson case, which he had done for a fee of $500. That intermediary then negotiated with Osborne with an agreement reached whereby Osborne would pay Yeandle, through the intermediary, a sum of $500 to achieve a hung jury in the Rosenheimer case. The money was handed over but the bills were marked as Osborne had informed the police beforehand and the authorities were aware of the negotiations and supposed agreement. Both Yeandle and Timondoffer were arrested.

Another surprise announcement about Nan came to the public's attention in December 10 when a statement was issued that Patterson was then Mrs. Sumner Prescott. When the announcement was made she was living with her new husband at the Waldorf Hotel in Seattle. Sumner Prescott was described as a captain in the Spanish-American war, and was employed by the Vulcan Iron Works. Commented Nan; "All I ask from Seattle is that it leave me alone. I want to live my life quietly, and without disturbance, as long as I leave it alone. It can't possibly interest anyone else – it's my own affair. I want Seattle to forget about me." Sumner was the son of DeWitt Clinton Prescott, the president of the Prescott Company, manufacturers of machinery. It was thought the marriage had taken place in St. Paul, but no details were provided. It was also said that Nan would not be objected to by her new father-in-law.

Soon after Nan and the Smiths were released from incarceration the latter disappeared from sight. They were not heard from for seven years when it was noted, in October 1912, that J. Morgan Smith, described as "a tenderloin character" returned to the United States that month from Australia, with his wife Julia Smith. The pair "went into exile" (self-imposed) right after the trials, going to Australia. Morgan said he was engaged in the insurance business in Australia, "but without much success." He said he never discussed the Young case and his connection was "nothing but the result of Jerome's desire for notoriety." Then the Smiths, once again, disappeared from sight.

John Randolph Patterson, father of Nan, resident of Washington D. C., for over 50 years and a brother of the late United States Senator Willis Patterson of New Hampshire died in May 1915, aged 79 years. He had been ill for some five months. For many years he was connected with the United States Treasury Department, being supervisor of the architect division. He was also connected with the War Department and at the close of the United States Civil War he was instrumental in settling many claims held by the soldiers who had participated in that conflict. Later in his life he became interested in the real estate and insurance businesses but retired some eight years earlier. John was born in Lowell Massachusetts but came to Washington when he was about 21 years of age. He left behind one brother, Charles H. Patterson, a New York banker and seven children.

The two sons were Charles H. and Walter B. His five daughters were: Mrs. William L. Milburn; Mrs. E. J. Taylor; Mrs. Harriet P. Lowell (all three of Washington); Mrs. J. Morgan Smith (San Francisco); and Mrs. Sumner Prescott (Seattle).

Little was heard from Seattle about Nan, for a time. A brief one-line report in April 1913 stated that she "is leading a happy married life in the West." That a report surfaced from Cincinnati that Nan had been named as corespondent in the amended divorce petition of Mrs. Viola Dillingham of that city, who charged that her husband Frank A. Dillingham, patent medicine manufacturer, traveled with Nan on a steamboat from Seattle to Alaska in 1913. But just three weeks later in Cincinnati a motion was filed in domestic relations court there to strike out the name of Nan Patterson from the amended divorce proceedings. It was shown that it was a ringer who had used the name of Nan Patterson. Attorneys representing Mrs. Samuel Prescott of Seattle, presented proof Nan could not have been in the company of Dillingham at the time in question. Nan was blameless in this case but as so often had happened in the past, got the blame anyway, although in this case it was corrected.

Mrs. Agnes A. Young was arraigned in Special Sessions Court in Yonkers New York on September 23 1921 on a charge of assault brought by Francis S. Feich, also of Yonkers. Mrs. Young was Nan Patterson. Feich claimed that on July 29 Mrs. Young ripped her shirt, threatened her with a revolver and threw stones at her during a dispute at the home where the two resided. Feich was Nan's landlady. The story went that on July 29 Mrs Young was doing her laundry when Feich said she wanted to use the washtubs for her family and in the discussion that followed an altercation broke out between the two women. When the case was heard in court, on December 11 1921, Mrs Young said that in that altercation Feich grabbed Nan, pushed her back and choked her. Because complainant Feich did not show up in court Judge Charles W. Boote dismissed the case.

The final appearance of Nan Patterson in print, that I could locate, was in February 1922. It was reported that on February 13 the former "idolized *Floradora* girl lives in poverty in a hut near Yonkers. Her name came back to the front pages the other day when she was arrested for fighting with a band of gypsies encamped near her 'wretched hovel.'" Her story was briefly recapped and the reporter concluded by writing; "Then began the descent. A few years ago she was noticed, now and then swathed in black, in the cheaper cafes on the fringe of Broadway. Then the backwaters of life closed over her and she was seen no more."

No one will ever know what happened on that June 4 1904 morning. It was almost certain that Nan was not guilty of a felony. It was almost certain that Caesar Young entered that cab that morning carrying the gun that eventually caused his death. It was almost certain that Morgan Smith did not buy the gun and had nothing to do with the tragedy. It was certain that Hyman Stern did not sell the weapon from his pawnshop on June 3 1904. On the basis of a realistic assessment of the "facts," the few facts that were known, Nan Patterson should never have been brought to trail once, let alone three times. The fact that the jury was hung twice surprised most observers and was unexpected. Most had expected a fairly quick acquittal. The fact that no acquittal ever came had nothing to do with the state's case, which was abysmal for the understandable reason that they had no case, and everything to do with the status of the defendant and the overwhelming negative and hostile press assaults upon her. She was young, female, and had not lived or accepted the life of an obedient housewife. Those assaults continued upon her release from custody, after almost a full year in detention. Patterson's behavior, at times, did not help her own cause, but the lies against her from the media came so fast and furious that it was almost impossible to tell what stories, if any, contained even a little truth. Nan Patterson's personal life seemed to have deteriorated rapidly in the 1920s and it sounded as if she had been reduced to fairly serious poverty. Nan would have died long ago, however, I could find nothing in the public record about when that happened.

This portrait of Patterson was taken for a Washington D. C. newspaper just a few days after her release. She is in the yard of the family home in that city.

BIBLIOGRAPHY.

"A case of suicide or murder." *Deseret Evening News* (Salt Lake), Jun 4 1904.

"A Saturday sermon." *Topeka State Journal* (KS), Jul 6 1907.

"A tardy witness." *Washington Times*, Nov 2 1904.

"A woman's fight." *Seattle Star*, Mar 16 1905.

"Actress may summer in jail." *Sun* (NY), Jun 12 1904.

"Again at the altar." *Evening Star* (Washington), Sep 16 1905.

"Amusements." *Deseret Evening News* (Salt Lake), Sep 9 1901.

"Amusements of summertime." *Sun* (NY), Jun 26 1904.

Ad. *Paducah Sun* (KY), Jan 17 1902.

"An object lesson." *Pierre Free Press* (SD), Jun 8 1905.

"Another turf scandal." *Waterbury Evening Democrat* (CT), Dec 29 1903.

"Another Young witness." *New York Tribune*, Nov 3 1904.

"As money gives out." *Morning Astorian* (Astoria OR), Sep 6 1907.

"At the theatre" *Savannah Morning News* (GA), Feb 16 1902.

"Attorney Rand Welding chain about actress." *Washington Times*, Apr 25 1905.

"Back to her old ways." *Topeka State Journal* (KS), Aug 27 1907.

"Bail bond now ready to free Nan Patterson." *Washington Times*, Sep 27 1904.

"Bail for Nan Patterson." *Sun* (NY), Sep 2 1904.

"Bars to freedom stay." *Evening Star* (Washington), May 11 1905.

"Battle of suds ends in a clean victory." *Adrmoreite* (Ardmore OK), Dec 11 1921.

"Becomes faint in the courtroom." *San Francisco Call*, Apr 25 1905.

"Bellboy skips with her coin." *San Francisco Call*, Mar 16 1903.

"Big crowd sees Nan Patterson." *Evening World* (NY), May 29

1905.

"Birthday presents carried to her cell." *San Francisco Call*, Sep 13 1904.

"Blow to defense of Nan Patterson." *Minneapolis Journal*, Nov 24 1904.

"Bookmaker kills himself." *Lewiston Evening Teller* (ID), June 4 1904.

"Bookmaker shot in car." *New York Tribune*, Jun 5 1904.

"Bookmaker suicided," *Fargo Forum* (ND), Jun 4 1904.

"Bookmaker Young is laid to rest." *Washington Times*, Jun 7 1904.

"Bribery charge in murder trial; juror arrested." *Washington Times*, Nov 1 1910.

"Briefly told" *Washington Times*, Sep 15 1901.

"Broken in spirit and discouraged, Nan Patterson quits stage." *Fairmont West Virginian*, Jun 5 1905.

"Butchers row over their holiday." *San Francisco Call*, May 25 1901.

"Cabman loses memory about Nan Patterson." *Evening World* (NY), Dec 9 1904.

"Caesar Young fails to book." *San Francisco Call*, Mar 2 1904.

"Caesar Young is killed in a cab." *St. Paul Globe*, Jun 5 1904.

"Caesar Young killed in cab with actress." *St. Louis Republic*, Jun 5 1904.

"Caesar Young, the California turfman, slain while riding in cab with actress." *San Francisco Call*, Jun 5 1904.

"Caesar Young was infatuated with fair young actress." *Fairmont West Virginian*, Nov 16 1904.

"Called by Grand Jury." *Evening Star* (Washington), Apr 6 1905.

"Can a moral, upright chorus girl succeed?" *Cairo Bulletin* (IL), Nov 27 1904.

"Can't identify Morgan Smith." *Sun* (NY), Apr 27 1905.

"Can't stop Nan Patterson." *Sun* (NY), May 29 1905.

"Case against Nan all in." *Sun* (NY), Dec 12 1904.

"Characteristic views of counsel prosecuting Nan Patterson."

Savannah News (GA), Dec 3 1904.

"Charge is dismissed." *Evening Star* (Washington), Apr 14 1905.

"Charge of a plot is ruled out by court." *Evening World* (NY), Dec 14 1904.

"Corbett to the rescue." *Evening Star* (Washington), Sep 27 1904.

"Coroner commits *Floradora* beauty to Tombs prison." *New York Tribune*, Jun 5 1904.

"Corroborates Meyer in story of shooting," *Evening World* (NY), Jun 9 1904.

"Court angry over fake interviews on Nan Patterson." *Evening World* (NY), Dec 12 1904.

"Court stops Nan Patterson performance." *Evening World* (NY), May 30 1905.

"Criminal bar is aroused by Judge Davis's criticisms." *Evening World* (NY), May 18 1905.

"Criminal courts going again." *Sun* (NY), Oct 4 1904.

"Crowd sees Nan Patterson." *Evening World* (NY), Feb 28 1905.

Currie, Barton W. "Nan weeps in arms of aged mother." *Evening World* (NY), May 13 1905.

"Davis's speech makes talk." *Sun* (NY), May 17 1905.

"Day before Young was shot." *Sun* (NY), Nov 24 1904.

"Death shot in cab." *Sun* (NY), Jun 5 1904.

"Defends Nan Patterson." *Deseret Evening News* (Salt Lake), Dec 14 1904.

"Delay in Nan Patterson." *Evening World* (NY), Jun 25 1904.

"Denies Nan Patterson confessed." *New York Tribune*, May 19 1905.

"Detectives seek owner of pistol." *Washington Times*, Jun 8 1904.

"Didn't free Nan Patterson." *Sun* (NY), Sep 7 1904.

"Discredits the theory of suicide" *San Francisco Call*, June 6 1904.

"Does it pay to be good?" *Los Angeles Herald*, Jun 18 1905.

"Drawing to a close." *Evening Star* (Washington), May 1 1905.

"Entered court jauntily." *Evening Star* (Washington), Nov 16 1904.

"Eva Booth says Nan Patterson is not guilty." *Evening World* (NY), May 6 1905.

"Events in the West." *Deseret Evening News* (Salt Lake), Oct 4 1897.

"Evolution of a new type of show girl." *Appeal* (St. Paul), Jun 1 1907.

"Evolution of a new type of show girl." *Appeal*, (St. Paul), Jun 1 1907.

"Expected trump card." *Evening Star* (Washington), Apr 26 1905.

"Expects her freedom." *Evening Star* (Washington), Jun 15 1904.

"Experts are on the stand." *Salt Lake Tribune*, Nov 24 1904.

"Failed to get her freedom." *Evening Star* (Washington), Sep 7 1904.

"Failed to identify." *Evening Star* (Washington), Apr 26 1905.

"Fair brides of the spring." *Evening Journal* (Wilmington DE), Apr 17 1901.

"Family accepts Nan Patterson." *Hawaiian Star* (Honolulu), Dec 24 1910.

"Far too timid says her chum." *Washington Times*, Jun 6 1904.

"Father fears insanity for Nan Patterson." *Washington Times*, Dec 29 1904.

"Fight indictment of Nan Patterson." *Evening World* (NY), Jun 13 1904.

"Fitted in her prison for stunning dresses." *Washington Times*, Nov 14 1904.

"*Floradora* girl flinches before prosecutor Rand." *Washington Times*, Apr 24 1905.

"*Floradora* girl gets a divorce." *San Francisco Call*, May 1 1903.

"*Floradora* revival recalls romances of original sextet." *Sun* (NY), Mar 21 1920.

"Floradora." wikipedia.org, accessed Mar 21 2020.

"For third time Nan Patterson called to bar." *Washington Times*, Apr 18 1905.

"Former Nan Patterson is accused of assault." *Evening World* (NY), Sep 23 1921.

"Fourth day of trial." *Evening Star* (Washington), Nov 21 1904.

"Freedom denied Nan Patterson after hearing." *Evening World*

(NY), Jun 7 1904.

"Freedom for Nan now near at hand." *Washington Times*, May 8 1905.

"Freedom for Nan Patterson near at hand." *Evening World* (NY), Dec 28 1904.

"Gay actress too gay." *Seattle Republican*, Jun 17 1904.

"Gossip of the stage and the player folk." *San Francisco Call*, Jun 11 1905.

"Grand juror at home." *Sun* (NY), Jun 19 1904.

"Grand Jury hears Patterson case." *Washington Times*, Jun 9 1904.

"Has no faith in Nan Patterson." *Los Angeles Herald,* Jan 3 1905.

"Held in Tombs." *Topeka State Journal* (KS), Jun 6 1904.

"Her celebration." *Spokane Press*, May 20 1905.

"Her life is a puzzle." *Evening Star* (Washington), Apr 17 1905.

"Horseman killed riding in a hack." *Rock Island Argus* (IL), Jun 4 1904.

"How Nan Patterson looked during the trial." *St. Paul Globe*, Dec 25 1904.

"How Nan Patterson witness describes the killing of Young." *Evening World* (NY), Apr 22 1905.

"I did not kill Caesar Young." *Evening World* (NY), Dec 19 1904.

"Important witness is arrested." *San Francisco Call*, Nov 26 1904.

"Injustice to actresses." *St. Paul Globe*, Jun 26 1904.

"Is Nan Patterson falsely accused." *Deseret Evening News* (Salt Lake), Nov 2 1904.

"J. Morgan Smith may go to court." *Evening World* (NY), Jun 11 1904.

"Jerome bolts cage for Nan Patterson." *Washington Times*, Jan 1 1905.

"Jerome frees Nan Patterson." *Washington Times*, May 12, 1905.

"Jerome holds letters." *Evening Star* (Washington), Apr 4 1905.

"Jerome may retain Morgan Smith letters." *Evening World* (NY), Apr 24 1905.

"Jerome offered to free Nan." *Washington Times*, Nov 28 1904.

"Jerome ordered to give up all Nan's letters." *Washington Times*,

Apr 16 1905.

"Jerome says Nan Patterson can't go yet." *Evening World* (NY), May 9 1905.

"John B. Patterson dies." *Evening Star* (Washington), May 4 1915.

"Judge goes home, but will return to receive verdict." *Evening World* (NY), Dec 22 1904.

"Juror's action great surprise." *Washington Times*, Dec 24 1904.

"Juror's illness halts trial of Nan Patterson." *Washington Times*, Nov 26 1904.

"Jurors all chosen to try Patterson girl for murder." *Evening World* (NY), Nov 18 1904.

"Jurors who are trying Nan Patterson." *Savannah Morning News* (GA), Dec 16 1904.

"Jury not agreed." *Sun* (NY), Dec 23 1904.

"Jury of married men to try Nan Patterson." *San Francisco Call*, Apr 20 1905.

"Kill me! Cried Nan Patterson to a policeman." *Evening World* (NY), Nov 21 1904.

"Killed in a cab," *Evening Star* (Washington), Jun 4 1904.

"Lawyer muzzles Nan Patterson." Washington Times, Nov 4 1904.

"Leading the old life." *Arizona Journal-Miner* (Prescott), Jun 26 1907.

"Leave me alone that's all says Nan Patterson, here." *Seattle Star*, Dec 10 1910.

Leckie, Katharine. "Nan Patterson in court, a study of the accused girl." *Spokane Press*, Nov 21 1904.

Leckie, Katharine. "Nan Patterson tells of love for Young." *Evening World* (NY), Dec 19 1904.

"Letters showed on Nan Patterson." *St. Louis Republic*, May 6 1905.

"Los Angeles escapades." *San Francisco Call*, Jun 5 1904.

"Loved another woman." *Capital Journal* (Salem OR), Jun 4 1904.

"May indict Nan Patterson." *Sun* (NY), Jun 8 1904.

"May trace revolver's ownership." *San Francisco Call*, Jun 7 1904.

McIntyre, O. O. "Nan Pattersons many in Gotham, says

M'Intyre." *Washington Herald,* Feb 14 1922.

"Miss Patterson free" *New York Tribune,* May 13 1905.

"Miss Patterson meets managers." *New York Tribune,* May 18 1905.

"Miss Patterson to play." *New York Tribune,* Sep 2 1904.

"Missives reveal plot." *Evening Star* (Washington), Apr 5 1905.

"Morgan Smith gets here." *Sun* (NY), Apr 12 1905.

"Morgan Smith gives up fight, returns home." *Evening World* (NY), Apr 10 1905.

"Morgan Smith yet in hiding." *San Francisco Call,* Nov 16 1904.

"Morgan Smiths apply for writ." *Washington Times,* Apr 1 1905.

"Morgan Smiths are caught." *Sun* (NY), Mar 31, 1905.

"Morgan Smiths are much wanted." *Washington Times,* Jun 11 1904.

"Morgan Smiths in court; Nan Patterson faints." *Evening World* (NY), Apr 24 1905.

"Morgan Smiths not at capital." *Washington Times,* Jun 19 1904.

"Mr. J. Morgan Smith." *Deseret Evening News* (Salt Lake), Apr 15 1905.

"Mrs. Caesar Young married." *New York Tribune,* May 4 1909.

"Mrs. Morgan Smith with relatives." *Washington Times,* Jul 7 1904.

"Mrs. Nan Patterson." *Deseret Evening News* (Salt Lake), Jun 6 1904.

"Mrs. Nan Patterson." *St. Paul Globe,* Jun 10 1904.

"Mrs. Patterson will explain the tragedy," *Salt Lake Tribune,* Jun 12 1904.

"Mrs. Smith released." *Evening Star* (Washington), May 12 1905.

"Mrs. Young faces Nan Patterson." *San Francisco Call,* Dec 15 1904.

"Murder indicated by wound." *Sun* (NY), Apr 26 1905.

"Murdered in a hansom." *Times-Dispatch* (Richmond VA), Jun 5 1904.

"Must stand trial." *Evening Star* (Washington), Jun 17 1904.

"Name of Nan Patterson stricken from suit." *Day Book* (Chicago), Dec 1 1916.

"Nan bright and cheerful." *Evening Star* (Washington), Nov 16 1904.

"Nan makes denial." *Sun* (NY), Dec 20 1904.

"Nan may soon be free again." *Washington Times*, May 4 1905.

"Nan Patterson." *Evening Star* (Washington), Jun 22 1904.

"Nan Patterson." *Evening Statesman* (Walla Walla WA), Sep 8 1904.

"Nan Patterson." *Hawaiian Star* (Honolulu), Dec 23 1904.

"Nan Patterson." *Northern Wisconsin Advertiser* (Wabeno), Dec 15 1904.

"Nan Patterson again," *Herald and News* (Newberry SC), Aug 1 1905.

"Nan Patterson and the Smiths are free again." *Evening World* (NY), May 12 1905.

"Nan Patterson at odds with father." *Fairmont West Virginian*, Aug 31 1905.

"Nan Patterson bail." *Evening Star* (Washington), Dec 30 1904.

"Nan Patterson banished by police from Pittsburgh." *Evening World* (NY), Jul 27 1908.

"Nan Patterson bars aged men from jury." *Evening World* (NY), Dec 5 1904.

"Nan Patterson before a judge." *Savannah Morning News* (GA), Jun 8 1904.

"Nan Patterson case." *Evening Star* (Washington), Apr 12 1905.

"Nan Patterson court in riot." *Evening World* (NY), Apr 26 1905.

"Nan Patterson decides not to put in a defense." *Evening World* (NY), Apr 28 1905.

"Nan Patterson driven away by a woman." *Evening World* (NY), Aug 16 1905.

"Nan Patterson faces witness." *San Francisco Call*, Dec 14 1904.

"Nan Patterson feel sure of acquittal." *Fargo Forum* (ND), Mar 23 1905.

"Nan Patterson flees avenger." *Washington Times*, Aug 16 1905.

"Nan Patterson freed, would enter convent." *Washington Times*, Jul 4 1904.

"Nan Patterson gets many offers of bail." *Evening World* (NY),

May 5 1905.

"Nan Patterson gives advice." *Hawaiian Star* (Honolulu), Sep 22 1904.

"Nan Patterson goes back to old life; plays races." *Cairo Bulletin* (IL), Jul 24 1905.

"Nan Patterson goes on stage." *Los Angeles Herald*, May 17 1905.

"Nan Patterson hailed." *Spirit of the Age* (Woodstock VA), June 3 1905.

"Nan Patterson happy at last." *Evening World* (NY), Nov 14 1904.

"Nan Patterson has no admirer" *Evening World* (NY), Mar 6 1905.

"Nan Patterson hears of a new witness who says he saw Young shoot himself." *Evening World*, (NY)
          Apr 21 1905.

"Nan Patterson in her father's home." *Evening Star* (Washington), May 14 1905.

"Nan Patterson in high spirits." *San Francisco Call*, Dec 5 1904.

"Nan Patterson in the courtroom." *St. Paul Globe*, Nov 20 1904.

"Nan Patterson in trouble." *Deseret Evening News* (Salt Lake), Aug 26 1905.

"Nan Patterson indicted." *Sun* (NY), Jun 14 1904.

"Nan Patterson inspects chins, beards, feet of the talesmen." *Evening World* (NY), Apr 19 1905.

"Nan Patterson is a genuinely reformed woman." *Washington Times*, Jun 17 1906.

"Nan Patterson is a physical wreck" *Evening World* (NY), Jun 14 1904.

"Nan Patterson is calm under Rand's new arraignment." *Evening World* (NY), Dec 8 1904.

"Nan Patterson is denied bail." *Evening Bulletin* (Honolulu), Jan 6 1905.

"Nan Patterson is ill." *San Francisco Call*, Oct 7 1904.

"Nan Patterson is in town, but under cover." *Evening World* (NY), May 18 1905.

"Nan Patterson is now set free." *Evening Bulletin* (Honolulu), May 12 1905.

"Nan Patterson is put off for a day." *Evening World* (NY), Nov 15

1904.

"Nan Patterson is wounded teller's anxious friend." *Washington Times*, Apr 27 1909.

"Nan Patterson jury disagrees and the woman will go free." *San Francisco Call*, May 4 1905.

"Nan Patterson jury disagrees." *San Francisco Call*, Dec 24 1904.

"Nan Patterson jury is out." *Spokane Press*, May 3 1905.

"Nan Patterson likes her jury." *Washington Times*, Apr 20 1905.

"Nan Patterson likes Pittsburgh roadhouse." *San Francisco Call*, Jul 2 1907.

"Nan Patterson may be set free." *Washington Times*, Oct 31 1904.

"Nan Patterson more hopeful." *Washington Times*, Nov 17 1904.

"Nan Patterson must face jury." *Evening World* (NY), Nov 2 1904.

"Nan Patterson named." *Capital Journal* (Salem OR), Nov 11 1916.

"Nan Patterson now sees her freedom by habeas corpus." *Evening World* (NY), Jun 6 1904.

"Nan Patterson on verge of collapse at sight of skeletons shown." *San Francisco Call*, Nov 23 1904

"Nan Patterson pleads not guilty." *Waterbury Evening Democrat* (CT), Jun 21 1904.

"Nan Patterson quiet and happy." *Times-Dispatch* (VA), Apr 15 1913.

"Nan Patterson raved when taken back to cell." *Evening World* (NY), Dec 23 1904.

"Nan Patterson refused offer." *Evening World* (NY), May 17 1905.

"Nan Patterson reweds her divorced husband." *Washington Times*, Sep 16 1905.

"Nan Patterson seeks liberty." *Evening Star* (Washington), Aug 12 1904.

"Nan Patterson selects jurors." *Minneapolis Journal*, Nov 17 1904.

"Nan Patterson states husband still loves her." *Washington Times*, Aug 31 1907.

"Nan Patterson still a prisoner." *Fairmont West Virginian*, Mar 1 1905.

"Nan Patterson sure she will go free." *Evening World* (NY), Nov 24 1904.

"Nan Patterson tells her story." *Washington Times*, Jul 25 1904.

"Nan Patterson tells the story." *Washington Times*, Nov 2 1904.

"Nan Patterson to be an evangelist." *Seattle Star* Dec 13 1904.

"Nan Patterson to be tried anew." *Minneapolis Journal*, Nov 28 1904.

"Nan Patterson to stay in jail." *Evening World* (NY), Dec 31 1904.

"Nan Patterson trial." *Evening Star* (Washington), Nov 22 1904.

"Nan Patterson trial a farce comedy." *Fairmont West Virginian*, Nov 21 1904.

"Nan Patterson trial Nov. 15." *Washington Times*, Nov 7 1904.

"Nan Patterson up to old tricks." *Paducah Evening Sun* (KY), Jun 14 1907.

"Nan Patterson wants jury of married men." *Evening World* (NY), Apr 18 1905.

"Nan Patterson weds." *Paducah Sun* (KY), Sep 16 1905.

"Nan Patterson well known." *Salt Lake Herald*, Jun 10, 1904.

"Nan Patterson wins." *New York Tribune*, May 4 1905.

"Nan Patterson writes story of tragedy." *Washington Times*, Nov 19 1904.

"Nan Patterson, not indicted, gets hope from Grand Jury." *Evening World* (NY), Jun 9 1904.

"Nan Patterson's backsliding." *Goodwin's Weekly* (Salt Lake), Aug 5 1905.

"Nan Patterson's bail fixed at $5,000." *Indianapolis Journal*, Jun 7 1904.

"Nan Patterson's bail." *Evening Star* (Washington), Jan 5 1905.

"Nan Patterson's bail." *Evening Star* (Washington), Sep 1 1904.

"Nan Patterson's brother-in-law, J. Morgan Smith, caught at last. *Evening World* (NY), Mar 30 1905.

"Nan Patterson's brother talks." *Washington Times*, Jun 7 1904.

"Nan Patterson's case." *Evening Star* (Washington), Apr 6 1905.

"Nan Patterson's case." *Evening Star* (Washington), Dec 28 1904.

"Nan Patterson's case." *Washington Times*, Oct 19 1904.

"Nan Patterson's chance of liberty." *Bisbee Review* (AZ), Mar 9

1905.

"Nan Patterson's father." *Sun* (NY), Apr 8 1905.

"Nan Patterson's father may be drawn into net" *San Francisco Call*, Apr 6 1905.

"Nan Patterson's jury. *Evening Star* (Washington), Nov 19 1904.

"Nan Patterson's mother very ill," *Washington Times*, Jun 6 1904.

"Nan Patterson's path – a circle – leads her back to jail." *Seattle Star*, Aug 1 1908.

"Nan Patterson's plea." *Evening Star* (Washington), Aug 31 1904.

"Nan Patterson's poem." *San Francisco Call*, Dec 28 1904.

"Nan Patterson's rights." *Washington Times*, Feb 28 1905.

"Nan Patterson's sister." *St. Paul Globe*, Apr 4 1905.

"Nan Patterson's sister loses place." *St. Paul Globe*, Jul 19 1904.

"Nan Patterson's tour," *Spokane Press*, May 31 1905.

"Nan Patterson's trial." *Evening Star* (Washington), Nov 8 1904.

"Nan Patterson's trial delayed by injunction." *Washington Times*, Apr 17 1905.

"Nan Patterson's trial to wait on Smiths." *Washington Times*, Jun 22 1904.

"Nan selects three jurors." *San Francisco Call*, Apr 19 1905.

"Nan will return to the footlights." *Washington Times*, May 17 1905.

"Nan's jury still is deliberating." *Evening World*, (NY), May 3 1905.

"Nan's new life excites comment." *Salt Lake Tribune*, May 23 1905.

"Nan's sister on stand." *Evening World* (NY), Apr 27 1905.

"Near the end." *Topeka State Journal* (KS), Dec 21 1904.

"Nearly faints at sight of skeleton." *St. Paul Globe*, Nov 23 1904.

"Nerving herself to keep up." *Evening Star* (Washington), Nov 18 1904.

"New danger faces Nan Patterson." *St. Paul Globe*, Apr 2 1905.

"New *Floradora* sextet fair rivals of the old." *Evening World* (NY), Apr 1 1905.

"New Nan Patterson witness." *Sun* (NY), Dec 10 1904.

"New Nan Patterson witness." *Sun* (NY), Nov 18 1904.

"New witness saw Young kill himself in cab." *Evening World* (NY), Nov 17 1904.

"New worlds will be introduced in murder case." *Fairmont West Virginian*, Nov 21 1904.

"New York detective here" *Evening Star* (Washington), Jun 22 1904.

"New York's latest sensational cases." *Waterbury Evening Democrat* (CT), Jun 10 1904.

"Nine for acquittal." *New York Tribune*, Dec 5 1904.

"Noted hounds will meet in special stake." *San Francisco Call*, Nov 29 1902.

"Noted prison leaving New York coroner's court." *St. Louis Republic*, Jun 4 1904.

"On trial for murder of Young." San Francisco Call, Nov 17 1904.

"$100,000 fund raised for the Morgan Smiths." *Evening World* (NY), Apr 1 1905.

"Partner seeks to slay an actress suspected of killing bookmaker." *Indianapolis Journal*, Jun 5 1904.

"Patterson jury box full." *Sun* (NY), Dec 9 1904.

"Patterson jury under suspicion of being unfit." *Washington Times*, Nov 20 1904.

Patterson, Nan. "The Flower of the Tombs." *Evening World* (NY), Jun 29 1905.

Patterson, Nan Randolph. "Warning to girls." *Spokane Press*, May 18 1905.

"Patterson woman gets trial" *Capital Journal* (Salem OR), Mar 4 1905.

Pendennis, Emmeline. "I'm happy and trustful says Floradora girl." *Evening World* (NY), Apr 19 1905.

Pendennis, Emmeline. "Psychological make-up of the *Floradora* girl." *Evening World* (NY), Apr 22, 1905.

Pendennis, Emmeline. "The real Nan Patterson seen by feminine eyes" *Evening World* (NY), Apr 21 1905.

Pew, Marlen E. "Case against Nan Patterson is falling slowly to pieces." *Spokane Press*, May 2 1905.

Pew, Marlen E. "There's not a single mark of a criminal about Nan Patterson." *Spokane Press*, Apr 19 1905.

"Plays have been written for Nan Patterson." *San Francisco Call*, Dec 13 1904.

"Plea for Nan Patterson asks that she be freed." *Washington Times*, Dec 27 1904.

"Pleaded not guilty." *Evening Star* (Washington), Jun 21 1904.

"Pleads not guilty." *Topeka State Journal* (KS), June 14 1904.

"Plot, cries Rand." *Sun* (NY), Dec 14 1904.

"Point for Nan Patterson." *Sun* (NY), Apr 15 1905.

"Police have theory." *Capital Journal* (Salem OR), Jun 7 1904.

"Police trace the revolver." *San Francisco Call*, Jun 10, 1904.

"Police watch the jurors." *Washington Times*, Nov 28 1904.

"Politician puts up cost to save Nan Patterson." *Evening World* (NY), Apr 3 1905.

"Pretty Floradora girl must answer to charge of murder." *Tacoma Times* (WA), Jun 13 1904.

"Price can't find J. Morgan Smith." *Evening World* (NY), Jun 23 1904.

"Principals in New York's latest tragedy." *Minneapolis Journal*, Jun 8 1904.

"Pugilist to aid *Floradora* girl." *Minneapolis Journal*, Jun 8 1904.

"Put in defense today." *Evening Star* (Washington), Dec 19 1904.

"Rand charges a plot to murder Caesar Young." *Evening World* (NY), Dec 13 1904.

"Rand had Nan upon the rack." *Savannah Morning News* (GA), Dec 21 1904.

"Rand's absence delays Nan Patterson's case." *Washington Times*, Feb 28 1905.

"Rand's failure raises hopes of Nan Patterson." *Evening World* (NY), Nov 16 1904.

"Reasons for denial of bail." *Evening Star* (Washington), Jan 7 1905.

"Relative of Nan Patterson here." *San Francisco Call*, Oct 11 1912.

"Revolt against Nan Patterson." *Sisterville Review* (WV), June 3 1905.

"Revolver is traced to buyer." *San Francisco Call*, Jun 8 1904.

"Saddle and paddock." *Birmingham State Herald* (AL), Jan 3 1897.

"Saw Young shot." *Topeka State Journal* (KS), Jun 8 1904.

"Says bookmaker Young shot himself in cab" *Evening World* (NY), Jun 8 1904.

"Says he saw Young fire." *New York Tribune*, Nov 2 1904.

"Searching for Smith." *Evening Star* (Washington), Jul 7 1904.

"Seek J. Morgan Smith." *New York Tribune*, Jun 10, 1904.

"Seeking evidence in Young case" *Minneapolis Journal*, Jun 10 1904.

"Seeking to have Nan released under bail." *Washington Times*, Jan 4 1905.

"Seven jurors are sworn in." *San Francisco Call*, Dec 7 1904.

"Seventh juror chosen to try Nan Patterson." Evening World (NY), Dec 6 1904.

"Severe is the tension in Nan Patterson trial." *Washington Times*, Apr 30 1905.

"She is indicted." *Topeka State Journal* (KS), Jun 13 1904.

"Simple life for Nan Patterson." *Washington Times*, Nov 27 1905.

"Skating on thin ice." *Spokane Press* (WA), Dec 3 1904.

"Smith bought pistol." *New York Tribune*," Apr 25 1905.

"Smith returns to old haunts." *San Francisco Call*, Jan 27 1905.

"Smith's capture elates Mr. Rand." *Washington Times*, Mar 31 1905.

"Smith's flight stops Young case," *Washington Times*, Jun 10, 1904.

"Smiths are here." *Evening Star* (Washington), Jun 18 1904.

"Smiths hard to extradit5e." *Sun* (NY), Apr 3 1905.

"Solves mystery of hansom cab." *Savannah Morning News* (GA), Jun 9 1904.

"Stage door Johnnies." *Indianapolis Journal*, Feb 3 1895.

"Starts at $1,800 a week." *Evening Star* (Washington), May 14 1905.

"State rests in Patterson case," *St. Louis Republic*, Dec 16 1904.

"Still a mystery." *Topeka State Journal* (KS), Jun 8 1904.

"Story Nan Patterson would have told jury." *Evening World* (NY), My 6 1905.

"Suffolk inspects the Tombs." *Sun* (NY), Dec 18 1904.

"Suicide in a hansom." *Topeka State Journal* (KS), Jun 4 1904.

"Suicide or murder?" *Evening Star* (Washington), Nov 24 1904.

"Sunday's World." *Evening World* (NY), Jul 16 1904.

"Sure she held pistol." *New York Tribune*, May 16 1905.

"Surety bond of $20,000 refused for Nan Patterson." *Brunswick News* (GA), Sep 29 1904.

"Talks too much." *Evening Star* (Washington), Apr 8 1905.

"The famous cab tragedy." *Iron County Register* (Irontown MO), May 25 1905.

"The indictment of Mrs. Patterson. *Savannah Morning News* (GA), Jun 15 1904.

"The jury chosen." *Waterbury Evening Democrat* (CT), Dec 9 1904.

"The jury which will decide Nan Patterson's fate." *Washington Times*, Dec 11 1904.

"The man they need." Hawaiian Star (Honolulu), Jan 3 1905.

"The Morgan Smiths' remarkable flight from justice." *Washington Times*, Apr 16 1905.

"The Nan Patterson jury has disagreed." *Waterbury Evening Democrat* (CT), Dec 23 1904.

"The Nan Patterson jury has disagreed." *Waterbury Evening Democrat* (CT), Dec 23 1904.

"The Nan Patterson trial." *Evening World* (NY), Dec 23 1904.

"The Patterson case." *Evening Star* (Washington), Apr 18 1905.

"The Patterson case." *Washington Times*, May 12 1905.

"The Patterson trial." *Sun* (NY), May 17 1905.

"The Primrose Path." *Potosi Journal* (MO), Jan 4 1905.

"To solve a mystery." *Evening Star* (Washington), Jun 6 1904.

"Tragedy in a car." *San Francisco Call*, Dec 24 1904.

"3 jurors for Nan Patterson." *Sun* (NY), Apr 19 1905.

"Trial consuming Nan Patterson's health and vigor." *Washington Times*, Nov 24 1904.

"Trial is postponed." *Evening Star* (Washington), Apr 10 1905.

"Trial of Nan Patterson on murder charge." *Spokane Press* (WA), Nov 15 1904.

"Trying to free Nan Patterson." *New York Tribune*, Sep 28 1904.

"Trying to get a jury." *Evening Star* (Washington), Nov 17 1904.

"Trying to trace the pistol." *Sun* (NY), Jun 7 1904.

"$20,000 bail for Nan Patterson." *Evening World* (NY), Sep 1 1904.

"Two more offers to wed Nan Patterson." *Evening World* (NY), Nov 25 1904.

"Upon the rack today." *Evening Standard* (Washington), Dec 20 1904.

"Use letters of father against Nan Patterson." *Evening World* (NY), Apr 6 1905.

"Utterly false, says Nan of latest story." *Washington Times*, Sep 2 1907.

"Visit Nan Patterson in prison." *San Francisco Call*, Jun 9 1904.

"Vivid scene in courtroom." *Washington Times*, Nov 23 1904.

"Want to marry Nan Patterson." Seattle Star, Nov 25 1904.

"Wanted as witness." *Evening Star* (Washington), June 10 1904.

"Wealthy bookmaker killed" *Mexico Missouri Messenger*, Jun 16 1904.

"Widow of Caesar Young sails." *New York Tribune*, May 18 1905.

"Wilkesbarre does not want Miss Nan." *Press* (Newport News VA), May 29 1905.

"Will surrender." *Waterbury Evening Democrat* (CT), Jun 11, 1904.

"With Nan Patterson in the Tombs." *Sun* (NY), Feb 12 1905.

"Witness for Nan Patterson found." *Los Angeles Herald*, Jan 2 1905.

"Witnesses at Nan Patterson's trial." *Washington Times*, Dec 14 1904.

"Woman in the cab shooting held in Tombs without bail." *Evening World* (NY), Jun 4 1904.

"Won't have Nan at this theatre." *Evening World* (NY), May 23 1905.

"Wound self-inflicted." New York Tribune, May 2 1905.

"Wrongfully held." *Washington Times*, Sep 29 1904.

"Young a suicide, he says." *Sun* (NY), Nov 3 1904.

"Young commits suicide." *Evening Statesman* (Walla Walla WA), Jun 4 1904.

"Young may have died trying to save the woman." *Washington Times*, Jun 12 1904.

"Young owned a pistol." *San Francisco Call,* May 4 1905.

"Young promised to marry." *Sun* (NY), Apr 28 1905.

"Young tragedy told in court." *Washington Times*, Nov 22 1904.

"Young's widow builds tomb." *San Francisco* Call, Feb 24 1906.

"Young's widow testifies." *Sun* (NY), Dec 16 1904.

Ziegfeld, Florenz Jr. "The passing of the Johnny." *Washington Times*, Aug 28 1921.